Porch
PRESENCE

Porch
PRESENCE

Interior Design for the Exterior Room

— Sally Fennell Robbins —

Grove Weidenfeld
New York

A FRIEDMAN GROUP BOOK

Copyright © 1990 by Michael Friedman Publishing Group, Inc.

Published in the United States by
Grove Weidenfeld
A Division of Wheatland Corporation
841 Broadway
New York, New York 10003-4793

Library of Congress Cataloging-in-Publication Data
Robbins, Sally Fennell.
    Porch presence/by Sally Fennell Robbins.—1st ed.
        p.   cm.
    Includes index.
    ISBN 0–8021–1225–0 (alk. paper)
    1. Porches—Designs and construction—Amateurs' manuals.
I. Title.
TH4970.R55 1989
694'.6—dc20   89–33172
                                                                      CIP

PORCH PRESENCE
Interior Design for the Exterior Room
was prepared and produced by
Michael Friedman Publishing Group
15 West 26th Street
New York, New York 10010

Editor: Sharon Kalman
Art Director: Robert Kosturko
Designer: Marcena J. Mulford
Photography Editor: Christopher Bain
Photo Researcher: Daniella Nilva
Production Manager: Karen L. Greenberg

Typeset by BPE Graphics, Inc.
Color separations by Universal Colour Scanning, Ltd.
Printed and bound in Hong Kong by Leefung Asco Printers Ltd.

First Edition 1990

10 9 8 7 6 5 4 3 2 1

dedication

To my parents and husband John

acknowledgments

It's not surprising the number of people who are enamored by the concept of the porch and its quintessential qualities. I am deeply grateful for the time and interest given by Thomas H. Hodne, Jr., architect, professor, and dean of the faculty of architecture at the University of Manitoba, Winnipeg; Randall Whitehead, president, Light Source, San Francisco; and Stephen Mead, architect and designer, Des Moines, Iowa.

Expertise and thoughts were also contributed by many other individuals. Special thanks to Robin Dorrell, president of Design Link, New York; contractor Paul Milowicki of Armburst, PA; David G. Frye, Sherman-Williams, Sayville, NY; Don Colby, vice-president design, Tropitone Furniture Company, Sarasota, FL; and Ansteress Farwell, architecture consultant, New Haven, CT.

Also appreciated are the opinions and experience shared by architects Kenneth D. Narza, Planned Expansion Group, Inc., North White Plains, NY and Lester R. Walker, Woodstock, NY, as well as New York-based designers Gary Crain, Josef Pricci, and Peter F. Carlson.

Contents

Porch PRELUDES

If you grew up in a house with a front porch, you already know the special romance of a place where memories are made, and family and friends gather.

On a hot summer's day it provides a breeze, and during a rainstorm there's a cozy swing or wicker rocking chair in which to cuddle up and savor a favorite book. In the glow of the moonlight, the porch chaperons youth's countless goodnight kisses. And before sunrise the porch deck accepts the hard thud of the newspaper's arrival. Even when unoccupied, this timeless space looks genuinely eager to shelter and nurture.

The porch may seem like an old-fashioned idea that's more in step with the 1800s than with the turn of the twenty-first century. Today, however, discerning people with distinctive tastes are returning to the porch in traditional and nontraditional ways.

Porch additions, renovations, and restorations are coming back in full swing. They're also reappearing in new home construction. Porches may be enjoying a nostalgic revival, but experts say the allure is much deeper. People have been attracted *ad infinitum* to its many varieties for purely psychological reasons. "Porches appeal to people's emotions and imaginations," says architectural consultant Ansteress Farwell, of New Haven, Connecticut. She likens porches to bridges: "People love to see two things connected. With a porch it's a kind of magic; you're able to be inside and outside. You can have things but still be protected."

Porch Presence puts this roofed appendage to the house into perspective, from its early beginnings through evolution to porches today and their many species and functions. It provides guidelines and ideas specific to treating this exterior living space with the same attention given to interior design fundamentals. Included are some easy, hands-on projects to determine necessary repairs and special care measures to assure trouble-proof wear. With comfort and style in mind, the book also presents fresh and enticing design basics with a showcase of materials, furnishings, and accoutrements to outfit your porch with savoir faire. Nine high-style design studies provide informative ideas for transforming your porch into a room you will use year-round.

At the back of the book is a representative listing of manufacturers and sources that offer the finest in design and decoration for dressing your porch. After all, the porch is often the first room a visitor encounters. And wherever it is placed, it should be given the same level of design savvy and decor imagination as any other room in the house.

1

Porch
PERSPECTIVES

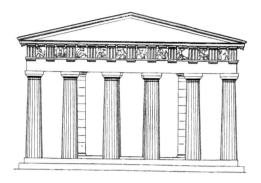

PORCHES YESTERDAY

The presence of the porch on the American streetscape has evolved from its ancient Greek birthright as a decorative and functional idea into extensive varieties and uses.

Derived from the Latin *porticus*, and more romantically called a *portico* by the Italians, this early edifice of architecture projected two columns topped by a pointed roof. It was intended as a shelter from sun and rain and also as a pleasant transitional element between the inside and the outside of a structure.

Over the centuries the porch has worn many epithets. Call it whatever you prefer.

The English borrowed from the Hindi and labeled it a veranda—a large, open porch with a roof that often extends across the front and sides of a house. Anglophiles may prefer the derivative from castles and palaces—a gallery, which at one time served as a long indoor hallway where family portraits were exhibited. This gallery idea was eventually translated by Colonial America to mean double porches.

Another more enchanting extraction is *piazza*, an Italian term that Americans in New England and the inland South interpreted as a large porch with a columned facade. One of

© Photri, Inc.

the grandest examples graces George Washington's Mt. Vernon home along the Potomac River, where his riverboat-traveling guests were received in the proper formality of the day.

As summer living spaces, European porches were adapted onto Southern homes, where, designed in a frontal position, they became solacing appendages for shade and cool breezes.

Up North, Yankee structures before the 1800s didn't have porches as we think of them, according to Thomas H. Hodne, Jr., an architect and educator of Minneapolis, Minnesota and Winnipeg, Manitoba. Instead, they had small, raised platforms, called stoops, at the entryway to their row houses; in the rear was the more private courtyard.

Above left: **This drawing shows an ancient Greek porch facade.** *Above:* **The grand piazza of Mt. Vernon, George Washington's home in Virginia, served as an entryway for riverboat traveling guests.** *Right:* **This southern home has a classical front porch that harkens back to its ancient Greek predecessor.**

Victorian architectural styles during the last half of the nineteenth century featured porch designs that were highly decorative and functional. This colorful example in Cape May, New Jersey (*left*), features double porches. The second floor porch is usually perched off of the bedroom and provides wonderfully cool breezes on steamy summer nights.

© Jerry Howard/Positive Images

As the new frontier moved west it was common for houses to have some type of porch. Once people felt more secure in their environment, they began moving outside.

"The basic purpose of that first real, more formal porch in our society was as an important communications element," says Hodne. Cities developed and once single-unit buildings emerged, "it was natural for people to have a porch. The classic front porch was to sit on . . . communicate . . . and to be seen and to see."

Perhaps the most instinctive period in the popularity of the porch occurred in the last half of the nineteenth century, as the Victorian style became a craze. In this type of architecture, the porch was designed to be both highly decorative and functional. Unlike the Puritanical confinements of the century or so before, people in the 1800s "were interested in going back to nature, and creating picturesque effects" for their homes, says Farwell. "People reached out into the landscape trying to unite buildings with nature."

Courtesy Dukes County Historical Society

Porches on Victorian homes were deemed so essential that they dictated the architectural style. Many porches were wide with deep, overhanging eaves and decorative balustrades. Examples of this can be seen here. This house (*above*) boasts a wraparound porch, while this Victorian-style cottage at Wesleyan Grove Campground in Oak Bluffs, Massachusetts, (*lower left*) has double porches.

© Jerry Howard/Positve Images

Many of the wood-framed cottages at Martha's Vineyard Campground look like Swiss chalets and have wide, extended porches.

Methodist campsites, located in rural wooded areas around America during the nineteenth century, produced communities with unusual building types and spatial qualities. Religious groups would attend these often-seaside resorts for back-to-nature revivals reconfirming their faith and rekindling the family bond.

Among the most famous of these campsites is Wesleyan Grove on the island of Martha's Vineyard, off the coast of mainland Massachusetts. Originally, visitors lived in tents, which eventually became very fancy. Later, from 1860 to 1890, according to Arthur Railton, of the Dukes County Historical Society, semipermanent structures were built.

These wood-framed cottages, dollhouse-like in scale, are closely knit along the narrow streets. Many look like Swiss chalets and have wide, extended porches attached to the middle space, which visually opens the area and softens the peculiar proportions. They were built extremely economically, yet their brilliant colors and gingerbread ornamentation give them a fantasy-like effect.

A porch was also built on the cottage's upper floor; according to Farwell this was used as an opening to move things like bedding in and out of the cottage because the staircase inside was too tiny.

Also, at many of the different campsites, the large ground-level porches served as a way for the public to view others' family life. People were judged by the community—a condition campsite participants had to accept. "During the day, these giant porches almost turned the house into a public stall," says Farwell.

Today, three-hundred cottages remain at this site; they are well-maintained and are a part of what is now called the Martha's Vineyard Campground, run by the association of the same name in Oak Bluffs.

In urban environments during the nineteenth century, the porch functioned as an extension of the home for both public and pri-

Many of the ground-level porches at the Wesleyan Grove campground (*left*) provided great public views. A new enthusiasm for fresh air made the sleeping porch (*below*) a popular berth.

vate social functions. It was a visually stimulating place that provided a good vantage point to look at everything and know what was going on in the neighborhood. And it served as a kind of holding station when unannounced visitors came to call.

Architecturally, one of the astute aspects about the nineteenth century, Farwell says, was the sensitivity to placing the porch in dramatic locations. Often, the porch was situated in a corner of the house to give a masterful feeling when gazing around the outdoors.

This was especially the case at the turn of the twentieth century. In the United States, for example, several factors contributed to people moving outdoors. The constraints of the Victorian era were loosening; one result was defiance of dark, dimly lit rooms. People were also inspired by the adventuresome and high-

spirited demeanor of President Teddy Roosevelt. At the same time, people were aroused into health consciousness because of polluted air in the cities, as well as the plight of tuberculosis, which was running rampant.

This enthusiasm for fresh air and hygiene thrust the porch from a merely decorative space into a functional one—a popular berth for sleeping. Often perched on the second floor—typically above another porch—sleeping porches provided a breezy retreat on steamy summer nights and were especially recommended for those suffering from tuberculosis. To keep the porch uncluttered, people often would rig beds that could be folded and stored, or rolled through a doorway.

By the early part of the twentieth century, porches were ubiquitous across the land—from urban to rural areas.

© Steven Brooke

This convertible porch is perfect for dining all year round. During the summer it catches the gentle breezes that flow in through the screens and the hallway, while in the winter it provides a dramatic backdrop to nature's show.

After World War II, however, new suburban areas began to wipe clean the old, and people wanted maintenance-free homes. Traditional architectural elements, like prominent porches, were an expensive upkeep headache. Many people stripped them off or enclosed them and converted them into rooms.

This mobile society preferred the new and modern; split-level homes with family rooms for television watching. Two-car garages were the status symbols of the times. People discovered the "California" way of life—the backyard patio and barbecue.

Unlike the security expressed in earlier single-family housing, there was an ambiva-lence about the place of the family unit on the streetscape. The fronts of new homes, in particular, became mere signboards as fastidious homeowners were preoccupied with mani-cured green lawns. With the exception of the South, the porch disappeared, and the back-yard patio and family room became the focal points for leisure-time activities.

It is only with the recent gentrification of our older, urban neighborhoods that people are rediscovering the joys of having a porch. Reviving them often makes a house more homelike; they provide a better sense of conti-nuity, can break up a large facade, and give the home a more textural quality.

© Martha Dimeo/Viesti Associates, Inc.

There are practical aspects, too. The energy crisis of the 1970s encouraged people to look for ways to reduce air-conditioning costs, and an open or screened porch provided cool breezes. Also, the trend in some regions toward smaller houses has made the convertible porch appealing because it can be easily winterized for indoor-outdoor use.

The porch, by whichever name you choose to call it—portico, veranda, gallery, or piazza—has had its share of ups and downs at the whim of changing lifestyles. Yet, few would debate its steadfast status as a pleasing architectural element. The porch continues to mature in the face of changing functions and designs.

Architectural elements, like these pointed windows (*left*), and design elements, such as comfortable wicker furniture with plush cushions (*below*) both add a particular refinement to the porch.

© William B. Seitz

© Allan Weitz

PORCHES TODAY

The popularity of the porch and the art of "porching" never lost its glimmer in some parts of America. Throughout the country there has been renewed interest in the porch, particularly since the mid-1980s. Also, the porch is making a comeback in housing developments in North America and Europe.

"There are some real strong movements, especially in Europe and Denmark," says Thomas H. Hodne, Jr., a proponent of porches for many years. He credits the influence of social planners for the renewed interest in porches. "Social planners have influenced designers to the point there are some real strong movements to make the communications porch an essential item of their housing structure," he says. "Porches are healthy options outside a walled surface area."

Many homeowners are reviving the porch because it can make an important stylistic statement about their homes. With this increased interest comes an increase in the number of styles a porch can take as a functional exterior living space.

Courtesy Pella/Rolscreen Company

Personal communication is regaining its importance for many who are tired of being engulfed by television. Having little time to spare, they realize there are better ways to spend it with the family.

There is also a greater outdoor awareness than in previous decades. Younger people, in particular, are taking a more traditional path in regards to understanding the roots of their neighborhoods and regions. More emphasis is being put on the home as a cocoon; a safe haven where comfort isn't compromised.

Unusual spatial configurations and contemporary styling are among the many elements in porch design. Windows are an important design component for beautiful indoor-outdoor vistas.

© Steven Brooke

Aesthetic qualities go hand in hand with the comeback of the porch in many regions around the country. And the types of additions being made for specific tastes and functions often reflect their location, from seasides to suburban neighborhoods, to the more private rural areas.

An example of a planned sense of neighborliness is Seaside, a resort "town" that began its development in the 1980s along the Gulf of Mexico in the Florida panhandle.

Seaside's homes (modeled after beach communities on Martha's Vineyard, Massachusetts and Charleston, South Carolina), town center, and evolving commercial sector are viewed as an important model for the direction of land development in the twenty-first century. The concept is already being adapted in the United States in several Eastern Seaboard cities from Baltimore, Maryland to Miami, Florida.

The archetype philosophy of Seaside was conceived by developer Robert Davis; its master planners were husband and wife architects Andres Duany and Elizabeth Plater-Zyberk of Miami. Designed as a cohesive small-town unit, Seaside's architectural style showcases the regional vernacular of the period before 1940.

Seaside's slogan is "The New Town. The Old Ways," and certainly there are vivid signs of the past: Pastel-colored clapboard houses with extensive front porches, three-foot-high (one-meter-high) white picket fences (no two can have the same pattern), and tin roofs are all among the mandates in the urban code to convey unity and harmony. Also, there is a set distance between the porch and sidewalk so passersby can easily strike up a conversation. And throughout the eighty-acre (thirty-two hectare) site there are gazebos, small piazzas, widows' walks, towers, and cupolas.

At the Seaside resort community near Panama City, Florida, every home must have a porch. A few of the many styles seen at Seaside include: a traditional back porch overlooking a new-wave sleeping porch (*opposite page*); a traditional front porch (*left*), and a screened-in Cape Cod-style porch (*above*).

Enhance the House Design

You're probably unfettered by strict design and construction guidelines and perhaps you don't want your porch to be a public space. So explore the architectural and practical possibilities. The porch can augment the design of the house while it provides the kind of shelter and functions you desire. If you're planning to add a porch to your existing home or including the space in new home development, consider the options available to you:

- wraparound (L-shaped)
- setback
- open
- enclosed
- semi-open (screened)
- convertible
- sunspace/greenhouse

© Steven Brooke

A wraparound, or L-shaped, porch can be scaled to the size and shape of a large house. The result can be softer lines with the added benefits of two vistas and exposures with varying degrees of privacy.

For smaller houses, a setback porch is often placed off the back of the house. It can provide a degree of privacy, protection from the elements, and a lovely view of the landscape. At the same time, a small setback porch can help retain the classic rectilinear frame of the home's architecture.

An open porch is the outdoorsy connoisseur of them all. It's a welcoming open-air room that offers some protection, yet its open sides entice garden fragrances and cool breezes. An open porch can add architectural interest to a flat and nondescript house, especially if it matches the house in color and type of roofing, and in wall construction. Supporting colonnades and balustrades provide a horizontal dimension to the home.

© Christopher Bain

A porch may seem old-fashioned, but it has many timeless options that can enhance the design of any house. Choices include a wraparound porch (*opposite page, above*) and a setback porch (*opposite page, below*). A back porch (*left*) offers protection from the elements, yet still offers a chance to relax in luxury while admiring beautiful views.

An enclosed porch serves up alfresco enjoyment year-round. Some homeowners may choose to convert their open porch rather than be chased indoors by inclement weather, or may initially have it built as an all-weather space, to use as a sitting room or entertaining area. For maximum openness and visual uniformity, wall areas can be made of double-glazed frames, as well as using tinted, double-glazed framing for the ceiling.

In keeping with the traditional porch family, many homeowners are adding a screened porch to their existing house or planning for it in new home construction. Besides providing a breeze and protection from the sun and insects, this semi-open variety is a flexible alternative to complete openness. The screened areas can be designed for removal during warm weather.

A relatively new alternative that has been gaining popularity is the convertible porch. It can be designed to be either open, screened, or glazed. The combination allows homeowners to convert their porch to adjust to the different seasons. This indoor-outdoor room is especially appealing with the trend towards smaller houses.

A porch can be screened all year long (*above*), completely enclosed by glazed inserts (*above right*), or convertible (*far right*), allowing fresh breezes in the warm months, yet remaining in use all year round.

Technology is playing an important role in the types of structures that can easily extend interior living spaces for year-round activities. In the early 1980s, a concept called a sunspace began catching on around the country.

The basic idea takes its calling from the historic conservatory, or greenhouse. The updated structure can serve as a source of solar heat, a place to garden, or it can interpret traditional porching activities into a wide-open, transparent living space that can be used year-round. You can even have a whirlpool installed.

Basically, a sunspace is a highly stylized, enclosed porch with a transparent roof and/or sides. The primary framing materials used to construct a sunspace are wood or aluminum.

There are many models and options, as well as custom designs available today. Besides additions to existing homes, sunspaces are being specified and integrated by architects and builders into new home construction.

There are many makers of sunspaces and prices for standard kits can begin at $4,000 and go as high as $50,000 depending upon size and elaboration. Additional costs entail building the foundation, materials, and installation. Extras can include electrical work and flooring installation. These costs can be estimated at about two-and-a-half times the price of the kit.

For a highly stylized look there's the sunspace—an enclosed porch with transparent roof and sides, framed in wood or aluminum. There are many models and options to choose from, and sunspaces can incorporate many other elements, such as a deck or balcony, into its design.

Courtesy Pella/Rolscreen Company

A sunspace provides an open living area for year-round use. It can be integrated into new home construction and can serve a special function, such as a breakfast nook off the kitchen area (*left*). Special blinds assure shade during the day and privacy at night.

Whichever porch option you choose, the interpretation will be a roofed structure attached to a house. There are also several cousins and hybrids to the porch. They are:

Patio. This often paved, ground-level space can be covered or unroofed and adjoins the back or side of the house.

Deck. A more modern rendition of the patio, it's often uncovered and willfully informal. The wood platform stretches into the landscape and occupies a whole or partial level of a home.

Balcony. A factor of high-rise buildings, this railed or balustraded elevated platform projects from the wall.

© Sandra Dos Passos

Courtesy California Redwood Association/photo: © Elyse Lewin

Popular hybrids to the porch are the patio (*above*), and the deck (*left*), a more modern and often uncovered area that stretches into the landscape.

Another porch cousin is more landscape-oriented. The celebrated **gazebo** from yester-century. Its small, roofed edifice can be open, screened, or serve as a latticework pavilion. For some housing styles, the gazebo concept can be incorporated into the redesign or expansion of a front porch.

What's germane among all these kin is their predisposition to please the desire for comfort. Porches today, whether bold new designs, or reminiscent of gracious favorites from the past—with latticework, colonnades, and spindles—evoke homage to a special place. You can easily imagine a lingering pace and simplistic pleasures.

Among other porch cousins are the balcony (*above*), an integral part of many row houses and apartment buildings, and the gazebo (*left*), a latticework pavilion that adds function and charm to the landscape.

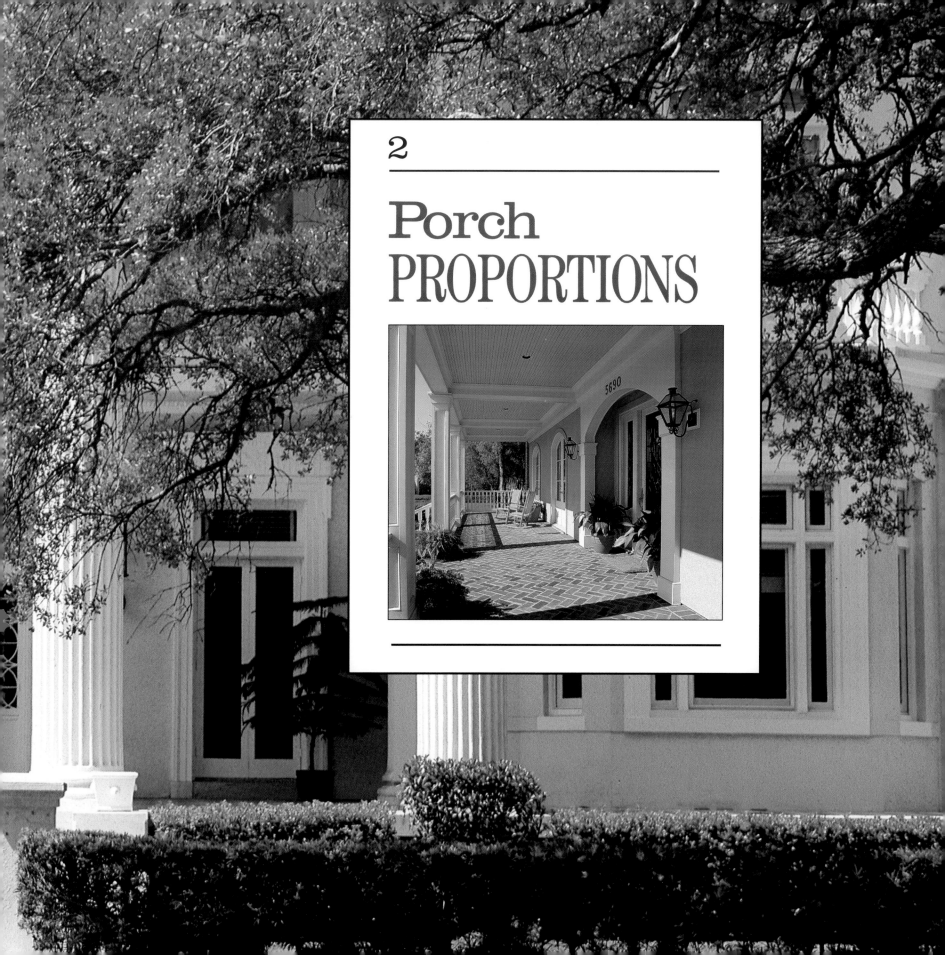

2

Porch
PROPORTIONS

© Donn Young

© Nancy Hill

Whether you want to add a porch to your home, renovate, or restore the existing structure, keep in mind that whatever is done will affect the resale value of the property. Besides an attractive and functional porch, you should demand quality planning and workmanship. It's important to feel comfortable about the investment you're making.

A frequent saying among the design community (and thought to be attributed originally to French novelist Gustave Flaubert) rightly applies here: "God is in the details."

Whatever is done, it's important to maintain the original detailing of the house. Even for a fairly simple job like screening a porch, the feeling of the space can be kept, for example, with modern, clean lines, or period styling.

Cape Cod, colonial, ranch, or bi-level. Whatever the architectural style of your home, the eventual design of the porch can be tailored to overcome a number of existing problems. For example, the addition of a porch can modify the shape of your home, giving it a better sense of scale; it can unify and control the irregularities in its structure; and it can provide texture and admit light at intersecting levels. Owners of older homes may want to create or renovate a porch in the style of the building's original architecture, such as English Tudor or Victorian. Or you can restore a porch to where it once stood.

For a plain housefront, which may only have a door stoop, add a portico to dress it up. In warm climates, create an outdoor room, partly sheltered and uncovered, to naturally extend the interior space, enabling you to enjoy those mild summer evenings and to get protection from the afternoon glare.

© Sandra Dos Passos

Left: **This new porch in Key West, Florida provides shade and a cool breeze on a hot day.** *Below:* **This Victorian wraparound porch has more than one exposure, taking advantage of the movement of the sun.**

When adding or renovating a porch, the facade—whether plain or ornate—should get special attention, such as geometric pillars (*opposite page, far left*) or fanciful designs (*opposite page, left*). The finished look should maintain the original lines of the home.

© Allan Weitz

PORCH PLANNING

When those first glimmerings of adding a porch enter into your mind, there are a number of preparatory steps to take before meeting with a professional.

First, develop a definitive wish list. This is the best starting point to program your needs and determine possible functions. Don't consider form so much at this point, but rather how this exterior living space will be used. Reflect upon your lifestyle and your family's lifestyle and the activities each member enjoys.

Also, when plotting your porch program, consider how the addition could affect the scale of your home or how it may affect the overall look of your home with the creation of a different, complementary style. "There are no absolute rules on how to design a porch, or where to place it," Hodne advises.

During this wish-list stage it's important to think ahead, too. You may want an open porch now, but then eventually have it enclosed. Such a "what if" thought process can make a difference later when it comes to local building codes and construction rules. Another important consideration is how public or private the space should be.

Tremendous sources for stimulating ideas about your dream porch are home design, decorating, remodeling, and residential architecture magazines, and books. You'll find the minimal investment worthwhile, even though many of your favorite photographs may not be applicable or within your budget limitations.

For restoration projects, research important traditions and origins about the house and its environs. You don't have to become an architectural history aficionado, but this kind of information will be valuable during the planning

© Sandra Dos Passos

© Carl M. Purcell

A porch serves as the crowning glory to any home. Here (*above*), the fanciful design of the porch adds charm to this Georgian home. *Left:* This porch turned an otherwise plain exterior into something special. When planning a porch take its uses into account: Will it be used primarily for relaxation and taking in beautiful views (*right*) or for dining (*far right*)?

Porch Functions

A porch can serve many functions. A few of the most popular follow:

- Entertaining;
- A dining/breakfast nook;
- A children's play area;
- A sleeping room;
- An exercise room;
- Solar collection;
- A sitting room.

Other purposes could simply be practical:

- Shielding the entrance;
- Providing shade to windows for cooler interiors;
- Enjoying the outdoors even during foul weather;
- Protection against incessant insects and bugs.

stage and, when implemented, will eventually enhance the value of your home.

The budget parameters are the final determinants you need to settle upon before sitting down with a professional. What you can reasonably afford will affect the overall scheme and scope of the project.

"Generally, people can't start with a minimum budget because they often don't know what a porch costs to build," says Robin Dorrell, president of Design Link, a New York–based consulting service that analyzes clients' needs and then locates the most appropriate design professional for the job.

If you want to get some idea of financial reality before you investigate hiring a professional, consider Dorrell's advice: "Have a contractor come in and tell him about the addition you're considering. Ask him what he thinks it would cost to build" the kind of porch you have in mind. Do this exercise with two or three local contractors and you'll have a clearer idea about what the ballpark figure might be. Sometimes the budget parameters indicate what has to be eliminated from your wish list. Be prepared for trade-offs.

Once you synchronize ideas for your porch with budget boundaries, it will be the role of the professional designer to interpret your needs, examine your home's structure, and decide the plausibility of making them work together. Sometimes there are existing conditions within the home's structure that may require unforeseen modifications of plans. Yet in other cases, there are cirumstances that are easily identified and figured into the layout.

Many professionals say there are no absolute rules about how to design a porch and where it should be placed. Specific purposes, however, can lend themselves to logical positions. For example, if you want a sleeping porch because you love fresh air in the summertime, it may be appropriate to have the porch located off the master bedroom. Or, if you intend to use

You have many options in the placement of your porch: Place it facing an enticing swimming pool (*opposite page*), a captivating landscape (*above, top*), or overlooking a beautiful oceanscape (*above*).

your porch for dining, situate it close to the kitchen for easier access.

Generally, placement of the porch can be on the street side of the house, facing the landscape, adjoining the back of the house, or set into a corner. Wherever the porch ends up, it should be accessible to an entryway.

Because comfort is important, consider the exposure your future porch will receive. Placing it on the north side of the house will shade it during the day; a southern exposure will furnish plenty of morning sunshine.

Be open-minded about design materials. Though many porches are made of wood or brick, there are a variety of effects that can be applied to many housing styles in aesthetic ways; much depends upon your design sensitivity. For example, Hodne suggests the "use of very contemporary materials for a very traditional house," which he says can be done "without destroying [the design]."

Also, there are many translucent materials today that enable porches to be built without reducing interior light while allowing good natural illumination in the exterior space.

Homeowners who are accomplished do-it-yourselfers with an aptitude for technical tasks may want to build their own addition or renovate an existing structure. If that's the case, experts advise a consultation with a local design professional before beginning the project. You may have missed something. A makeshift result can hurt the refinement of the house overall and detract from the property's value.

Also, check into important details, such as local building codes and zoning restrictions, about what can or cannot be added to your house. At the least, there may be a requirement for a building permit. And there may be varying requirements for setbacks (the distance from the front property line at which you can build an addition to a house) or rules for the width of side yards, if you plan to add a porch to the side of the house. And if a variance is needed, this request should be made to the zoning commission *before* the project begins.

Other conditions could be material specifications and necessary inspections. Also, you must be sure that the new structure won't disrupt utility or phone lines, and water, gas, or sewerage systems.

Be aware of these kinds of significant technicalities. If you're hiring a professional for the project, it's his or her responsibility to handle these details before any physical labor is begun. They're familiar with these matters and can

© Larry A. Brazil

quickly determine the specific limitations and requirements you will have on the porch you are planning to build.

During the planning phase is also an opportune time to retrieve the house's deed from safekeeping; check it to see if there are any easements that may affect your potential porch plans. Such a law permits another property owner to make use of the land you hold for a limited purpose. Also, there could be special rights-of-way for road passage that you were not previously aware of.

Wood is the most common design material for porches (*above*) but there are other, more contemporary, options available, such as concrete slabs (*opposite page*). No matter what material you use for your porch, the design should complement the house exterior (*right*).

© Christopher Bain

© Peter Gridley/FPG International

PORCH CHEMISTRY: CHOOSING THE RIGHT PROFESSIONAL

Some homeowners have the expertise to design and build their own porch addition or renovation. Many others, however, require professional help. If you will be hiring outside help, you may wonder if you should work directly with an architect or with a contractor. That decision depends upon the complexity of the project. Modest repairs and replacements for your existing porch may only require a general contractor. But, if your porch requires major structural rehabilitation, consider an architect, as they usually have a better background in engineering and design, compared with a general remodeling contractor.

© Sandra Dos Passos

Another option is the "design build" contractor who's experienced in structural design as well as building. This popular type of remodeling firm usually has professional designers or architects on staff, according to Robert Gluck of the National Association of Home Builders Remodelors Council.

In addition, you may want to consider hiring an architect who also builds.

Sometimes homeowners may want to have the architect develop the design plans and then have their local general contractor and his suppliers execute the job. Sidestepping the architect for the duration of the project often can

© George Goodwin

Carefully choose professional help when planning to add or renovate a porch. Consider whether the job is right for an architect, a contractor, or a builder who designs as well. Attention to detail is an important part of the job.

© Christopher Bain

© Photri, Intl.

cause regret afterwards. An important role of the architect is to assure that what you approved gets built in the manner you want it. An architect can make the difference between a porch that looks like an add-on and one that appears to be built with the original structure.

The Architect

Your first step in hiring an architect is to explore your options; don't accept just any firm.

Should you already have a good relationship with an architect, there's no need to investigate. Or, if your home is an architect-designed house built recently, you may want to contact the original architect for guidance; that person may be in the best position to design the addition or to make design suggestions.

Many other homeowners will have to start from scratch. References from friends and neighbors can be a good starting point, but there can be pitfalls. What was right—or not so right—about their professional help could prove different for your project. Also, contact owners in the area whose porches you admire. Find out who they interviewed and finally selected to design the addition.

There are many kinds of architects. Some are theorists who choose to pass up work before they'd do a project that's not to their lik-

© Hallinan/FPG International

ing. Others practice so-called "contextualism." They take an aesthetic position that a building should be designed for harmony, or in a meaningful relationship with existing elements. Their styles swing both towards modern and traditional projects. Then there's the stylistic architect who makes a similar design statement on every project.

Don't be concerned if the architect doesn't show you a string of porch photographs. Expertise in the design process is what's important. "Zero in on the way the architect works with materials and proportions things, whether

Since the porch can be the focal point of your home (*right*), the right architect can make the difference, so explore the options and choose the professional best-suited for the project.

Once you have chosen a professional and discussed your ideas with him or her, blueprints (*right*) will be drawn up that serve as the design specifications for your porch. A good, and honest, working relationship can bring exceptional results, such as this innovative porch (*opposite page*).

you're looking at a home or a restaurant," Dorrell advises. "Get a feeling for how that person approaches design."

Has the designer addressed similar issues in terms of functional complexity and design goal? How will he or she approach the project and who'll be working on it? Ask for references you can contact.

Another key factor in choosing a professional is the level of rapport. A successful project relies on a good working relationship between the client and designer. A comfortable chemistry can make the difference. The process starts with you as the client and what you want to be created. "The architect should take your ideas and add tenfold to them, provided your budget can afford it," says Dorrell.

If you'd prefer professional "matchmakers," Design Link offers a relatively new concept in consulting services. Based in New York, the agency has affiliations in Canada, Europe, and Japan. Its referral process differs from independent agents like Decorator Previews because it makes accessible more than just interior designers. There's a broad spectrum of talent, including architects, landscape architects, contractors, and lighting designers for residential and commercial projects. The collaborative resource enables clients to simplify and coordinate the structuring of their design package. For a minimal fee it provides guidance in establishing project priorities and budgets, finds the right firm for your specific needs, and monitors the project through its completion.

For other leads, check with the local chapters of The American Institute of Architects (AIA) and the National Home Builders Association (NAHB). Keep in mind, such organizations do not recommend member firms.

However you select an architect, be sure to meet with two or three designers to get various perspectives. The process will make clear why you relate to one more than the others. Get a sense for how seriously he or she listens

to your needs. The more questions they ask, the better.

During the selection process, be wary if candidates are unconcerned about costs. You should certainly be frank about money. Besides building costs, there's the architect's fee. It can be designated in one of three ways: a flat fee, an hourly rate, or a percentage of the construction costs.

Generally, for small projects like a porch, it tends to be easier if you agree on a flat fee or an hourly rate with an agreed-upon cap. The percentage calculation most often makes sense for very extensive and expensive projects. Also, it requires precise decisions of what those con-

struction costs do and don't include. Finally, this method, which can range from 10 to 25 percent, just "makes people nervous," says Dorrell. "They think the architect will make more money" by putting extra expenses into the project. This, of course, is not necessarily the case.

Once you've picked the architect who has your full confidence in translating the priorities on your wish list, and once you have drawn up and signed a contract, there's only one thing left to do: let go. Dorrell says to as-

sume Murphy's Law because it totally applies to architecture. "'What can go wrong will go wrong.' Expect it, and relax."

A useful guide on how to establish and maintain a special relationship between owner and architect is offered by The American Institute of Architects: "You And Your Architect." It details negotiation of agreements and pro-

vides a list of design services. See the source section, page 135, for more information.

Also, a brochure with advice on selecting a contractor, writing a clear contract, and resolving disputes, is available from the Remodelors Council of the National Association of Home Builders; for more information, see the source section, page 135.

PORCH CARE: EVALUATE REPAIRS & REPLACEMENTS

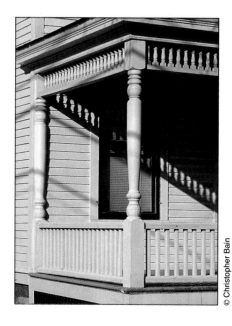

© Christopher Bain

Posts and related woodwork (*left, below, and opposite*) are among the first areas that deteriorate. Don't take shortcuts; slow the process by replacing rotted areas.

Even if you're not a handy person, there are some basic inspection steps you can do to determine the shape of your porch and what may need to be repaired or replaced. Here's a simple process to evaluate the extent of what may need to be done.

© John Reis

Check for deterioration and decay

Examine floor, railings, posts, and related woodwork for disintegration and look for loose mortar. Decay happens faster on older porches, compared with newer ones, because of weather exposure. And many older porches were built before the advent of treated lumber.

"When looking for decay, check where wood is against another piece," says general contractor Paul Milowicki, of Armbrust, Pennsylvania. For example, the setting of the post adjoining the porch deck, where moisture often gets trapped. "When you scratch around the paint there may not be anything apparent, but problem areas aren't easily visible."

Repairing problem areas with patchwork may be a short-term solution, but a homeowner is better off replacing parts of the porch that may be rotting underneath the surface. "Once the decision is made to repair a porch, we often find the condition is worse than it was thought to be," when the undersurface is examined, says Milowicki.

Assure supports are safe

Check how the newel posts (the posts supporting one end of a handrail at the top or bottom of the stairs) are secured to the porch floor. These may need to be replaced or refitted. Also examine the roof-support columns. These are susceptible to disintegration at their bases. Usually there aren't problems at the top portions of the column.

An easy way to repair the base and to slow the decaying process is to remove the bad part. First take the weight off the post with a screw jack and metal pole. Then remove the decayed portion and replace it with another block of wood, says Milowicki. For example, a two-by-four can act as a shim, or wedge, when cut in

© Christopher Bain

© George Goodwin

49

© Christopher Bain

© Jerry Howard/Positive Images

the shape of the post. This remedy is especially good for repairing a post that is set on a concrete floor slab.

Take Sound Frame Measures

Look for sags in the roof because they are good indicators of a deteriorating frame. "The roof is the best indicator to determine if the substructure is out of level," says Milowicki. If it is, determine if posts have sagged at the deck to cause the roof to sag. Then, he advises checking the deck. "Most porch decks are not perfectly level; they slope, so water can run off the deck."

The roof, however, should have been built

level. Be sure the supports from the ground up haven't begun to collapse. "Generally, if there's any noticeable slope running crossways from the slope of the house, there's a good chance of a problem area," he says.

Troubleshooting steps

Notice if the showing boards of the steps are loose, or if they seem unstable or unsafe. The top part is most often where major replacements are needed; the main supports deteriorate first, especially if located in an unprotected area. "The damage can usually be seen where one piece of wood contacts another," says Milowicki.

To ensure that your porch has a long and healthy life, follow these safety precautions: check the roof line for sags—it should be level (*far left, above*); check the posts, especially where they are attached to the roof (*far left, below*), as this is the place rotting can start; and always keep an eye on the stairs (*left*)—they can become unstable or unsafe. Always sweep leaves and snow off of the steps to prevent rotting.

© George Goodwin

Check for moisture

"The major enemy is rain," notes Milowicki about moisture problems, which can disintegrate wood. Although water dries and nothing appears on the surface, eventually dampness can become trapped in the joints, between the floorboards, or collect around the bottom of the porch posts, or wherever the wood meets the ground. "Once moisture is trapped, that's when a lot of insect decay starts," says Milowicki. "Termites need water, too, and they build trails to the ground to get water."

To help protect against moisture, he recommends sealing the seams of the posts that meet the wooden floors with a silicon caulking.

Open and semi-closed porches are subject to extreme climates and temperatures as well as insects and grime.

Be cautious about preserving them because the outdoor exposure can eventually take a toll. Negligence can transform slight renovations into major ones.

Whatever the age of your porch, there are several routine measures to help assure its trouble-proof wear.

Clean Sweeps

Be sure to remove dirt from the steps and floor, especially during non-use seasons. Otherwise, protective finishes will erode more quickly and encourage moisture getting into the wood flooring.

Don't allow snow to build up. Use a sizable, stout broom. Avoid the temptation to use a metal snow shovel because the blade can rip the wet floor grains.

Dry rot (*left*) can be caused by water damage that has collected over time around the foundation. By taking precautionary steps your porch can stay beautiful and healthy (*below*).

It's important to finish woods with a protective coating of some kind. Eventually, weather elements deteriorate paint requiring repainting when the old finish has worn thin (*below, right*).

Safeguard Woods

New porch flooring requires protection, but don't apply anything until about six months after construction has been completed. Pressure-treated woods and cedar and pine are not porous when fresh. They require a period of weatherization before they can adequately absorb any finish.

"It's important to do something to the wood. Although woods are generally treated with chemicals, they'll eventually rot if a coating is not applied," advises David G. Frye of Sherwin-Williams, Sayville, New York. Options include a clear coating that contains a preservative, an exterior stain, or paint—an oil-based exterior primer topped with a latex or oil-based finish coat.

As a surface coating, paint doesn't wear as well as an oil-based stain or a clear coating, which will be absorbed into the wood pores. Also, if paint is not correctly applied, there can be peeling or moisture problems.

"A stain or a clear protective coating with mildewcides and wood protectors will help prevent eventual rotting," Frye says. "Recoat every two years because it'll wear thin," due to weatherization and use.

If your porch is already painted, don't repaint needlessly. Dense, excessive paint buildup can cause the covering to crack and/or peel. Frye recommends repainting when the old finish has worn thin, or reveals bare wood.

© Christopher Bain

© Nancy Hill

Examine Flashings

Examine the flashings, or the materials used to cover and protect certain joints and angles of your porch. For example, where the roof converges with a wall. Snow and ice can raise the lower edge of the flashing from the roof plane. This can lead to leakage. Use binoculars to get a close look at the situation without climbing a ladder. Or, get a view of the roof flashing from the vantage point of the second floor of your neighbor's house.

© Nancy Hill

Pest Control

Property-damaging pests cause nearly one billion dollars in destruction a year. And harm done by termites alone affects two million homes annually, according to the National Pest Control Association.

Subterranean termites are common throughout most of the United States, even in the far northern states and some areas of southern Canada as well as in Mexico. With wood as their main diet, they tend to feed on piers and supports, foundation walls, and framing, among other areas.

A subterranean species, the formosan termite, is a problem in a scattering of United States localities, including Hawaii; Houston and Galveston, Texas; Charleston, South Caro-

lina; New Orleans and Lake Charles, Louisiana; and in several locations in Florida. Nicknamed "super termite," this breed moves through barriers such as masonry, concrete, and metal to get to the wood.

Other common pests throughout North America include carpenter ants and carpenter bees; both species excavate wood for a nest rather than actually consume wood, but carpenter ants are more destructive. If left unchecked, these colonies can weaken timbers to the point that they need repair or replacement. Telltale signs of infestation are small piles of wood chips.

Carpenter ants, most common in the Northeast and Pacific Northwest, prefer moist wood and nest in hollow doors, wall voids, areas between the roof and the ceiling of flat deck porches in hollow porch posts, and doors and window frames.

The presence of carpenter bees, although not considered a major pest of structures, can become quite annoying, according to the NPCA. They're most likely found in areas where wood is unpainted or lightly stained, or on roof trim and siding. These brightly colored insects excavate their nests in many different species of wood, but apparently prefer to infest softwoods, which are easy to hollow, and some hardwoods that have softened because of weatherization. For an indication of carpenter bees, look for little, round symmetrical holes in the wood.

When adding a porch, be sure to have the new foundation area pretreated with termitecides by a professional exterminator. And make sure cracks and openings throughout the foundation structure have been tightly sealed.

The insecticides an exterminator injects into the soil create a barrier. If your house has been treated recently, you should have it redone once the soil for the new foundation has been dug and retrenched. Such disruptions will destroy the barrier previously established.

The underside of the porch framing (*left*) is where termites tend to feed. Take a close look to assure that there is no infestation. While certain areas may seem secure from pests (*right, above*), there may be consequences to having lush, shrubby landscape too close to the open exterior of the porch (*right, below*).

To have an existing area inspected, contact a licensed pest control company to check all visible and accessible sections of the structure. Any evidence of infestation will be listed on a specified form. He won't be able to detect the situation behind walls or paneling, into voids of cinder block walls, or under carpeting.

If there's evidence of infestation, the company will recommend appropriate treatment for control. For termites, a treatment is usually warranteed for a year or longer. If an infestation is found during this period, the company will re-treat your home at no charge.

Although lush, wooded, and shrubby landscapes are often preferred settings for porches, consider the consequences: an open invitation for voracious pests to cross over and visit. And when you finally decorate you may want to rethink having freshly chopped logs neatly stacked, awaiting fireplace consumption.

© Jennifer Levy

3

Elements of PORCH DESIGN

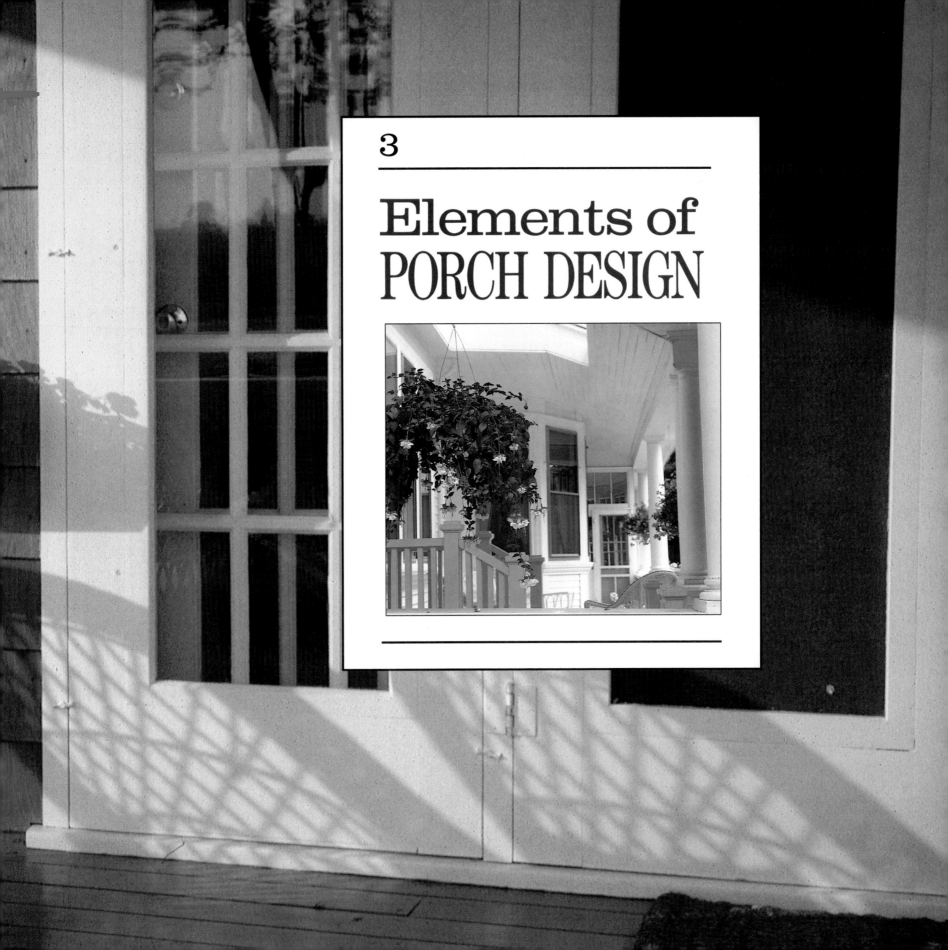

© Ron Chapple/FPG International

Unlike any other room in your home, the porch functions as a bridge to the outdoors. Thus, the design elements included in it should interpret a more carefree and self-expressive ambience. "Porches are a luxury space so you can treat their character differently—more whimsically," advises interior designer Peter F. Carlson of New York City and Stonington, Connecticut.

No matter if the porch is intended for year-round or seasonal use, you must plan the design elements carefully because they can help control the environment of this exterior room.

Key design elements requiring attention to detail are the windows and doors, and lighting, heating, and ventilation, if the space will be enclosed. Some factors, of course, can affect electrical considerations, too. Awnings, lattices, columns, and railings with supporting balusters and spindles are also architectural ingredients you may want to specify.

If you intend to hire an interior designer to translate your decorating tastes and needs, bring this professional into the project as early as possible so that he or she can work with the architect or design contractor you've selected.

Courtesy The Atrium Door & Window Company

Windows and doors (*above and right*) are important design elements for any porch. The type of door you want should be considered early in the planning stages.

WINDOWS

Windows in various shapes and sizes are significant elements that can help dictate how well the porch integrates into the overall design of the house.

For remodeling and porch additions, windows should be chosen based upon the design elements you want to express, recommends Stephen Mead, an architect and designer whose Des Moines, Iowa-based firm does a lot of porch construction nationwide.

© Peter Paige Assoc.

"The window becomes a design element relative to the kind of architecture," Mead says. "If you want something that tends more to the traditional side, we'll use some double-hung windows." For a neoclassical look he recommends a blending of window types. If contemporary is the style mode, he suggests casements or awning windows with a fixed unit over it.

Generally, he believes bow or bay window applications aren't suitable because they dilute the "porchiness" feeling. Rather, they're apropos in a more interior section of the house like the dining room.

Circlehead windows are especially popular for enclosed porches, Mead says. As visual accents, these can be used repeatedly with operable window units below them.

In enclosed porches, windows can provide important ventilation at the floor area—for ex-

ample, a ribbon of awning windows that run low to the floor with fixed glass above. These often can be topped by transoms, or windows above a crosspiece. Windows present an interesting correlation between two sides of exposure; from the interior of the house to the outside, and from the exterior room to the indoors. Also, if a porch is fenestrated, there's one side that's expressed exteriorly while the windows of the abutting structure of the house become the interior side of a porch wall. "It's almost a sunroom sort of application where we may or may not glaze the ceiling," Mead says. This floor-to-ceiling effect can be dramatic as well as practical for airflow.

"We like to get low floor and high wall ventilation rather than windows that simply open out or double-hungs that slide up and down for typical airflow," Mead says. "We use those ventilators as a design element to wrap around, develop strong horizontal lines, or maybe break them with some very strong verticals depending upon what the architecture is doing."

Many standard stock windows, such as casements, awnings, and some double-hungs, offer an interior screen made of fiberglass as an integral part of the system. If you want windows that can be converted to all screens or all glazing, you'll want a custom function. The appropriate screen depends upon the climate and orientation; they vary from sun screens to typical meshes.

"It's a storm window–type system with custom screening for the porch," Mead says. The screens are covered in the colder months, and the glazed area can be taken out and stored during warmer months.

"You don't have that availability of the screen open all the time with a standard stock window because part of the window will be closed down," Mead says. Also, it will have to be in an opened position, which can block breezes as well as views because of the vertical rail obstruction.

For enclosed porches there are many window options that allow only natural light to filter through. You may decide that simple glass windows (*far left*) better suit your style, or that small flourishes, such as circlehead windows (*left*) will add that special touch. The many shapes, styles, and sizes available will help dictate how the porch integrates into the design of the home.

Window Terms

AWNING. This window has one or more sashes hinged at the top so it tilts outward. Available with a low-maintenance exterior in aluminum with baked enamel finish. It uses a mounted, scissor-, or hinge-type cranking system to open and close. It is easy to clean and offers good ventilation. Can be used in combination with casement windows.

BAY WINDOW. Usually arranged with a large fixed center window and flanking vent units that have operable sashes joining the house wall at a 45-degree angle. Often designed with window seats or as a full-height bay. More appropriate to an interior room than to a porch.

BOW WINDOW. Vent-size units are installed on a radius to lend a feeling of greater spaciousness inside and traditional flair outside. Similar to bay, except sides curve rather than extend at the angle. Typical radial bows are formed using four to six casements. They are more appropriate to an interior space, such as a dining room.

CASEMENT. A type of window with sash openings on hinges that are attached to the upright side of its frame. Usually has lever or crank-type operator. Wood construction. Low-maintenance exterior available in aluminum with baked enamel finish. Can be used in combination with awning windows.

CIRCLEHEAD. A type of window unit available in different circular and ellipse shapes, as well as arch and cathedral-type configurations. Can be

© Phillip H. Ennis

© Phillip H. Ennis

sized to use in combination with casement and double-hung windows as well as doors. Available with low-maintenance aluminum exterior. Optional wood muntins may be fixed or removable for easy cleaning. Besides standard bars, special sizes and custom arcs are available.

DOUBLE-HUNG. This type of window has two vertically sliding sashes, each closing a different part of the window. Wood construction. Low-maintenance exterior available in aluminum with baked enamel finish. Can have pivoting sash and optional snap-out wood muntin bars to make window washing safe and easy. Sashes can be of equal size, or the upper sash can be larger than the lower one.

FIXED-GLASS WINDOW. This window doesn't open, as the name implies. There are a variety of shapes. Often used with other window types that are operable.

HOPPER WINDOW. Casement with sash hinged at the bottom instead of the top. It's usually used for below-grade basements because of poor ventilation and accessibility to rain.

JALOUSIE. This window features movable glass slats that can be adjusted to admit light and air but exclude rain and rays of the sun. Difficult to clean and insulate.

MUNTIN. A bar that holds the edges of window panes within a sash. Also called a sash bar.

SASH. A fixed or movable framework in a window or door into which panes of glass are set.

DOORS

There are countless styles of entry doors with frames made of wood, steel, and even fiberglass. Many offer glazed panels or transoms made of various kinds of glass, custom wood detailing, scrolled lock rails, moldings, period grilles, and leaded glass.

Among the types of doors appropriate for porches are traditional French doors with an in-swing or an out-swing, sliding glass doors, and traditional French sliding glass doors. The choice of door you use will depend upon personal preference and design factors. French doors are particularly appealing when they open onto a porch from the interior space.

Courtesy Pella/Rolscreen Company

© Jennifer Levy

Compared with sliding glass doors, Mead says French doors lend a friendlier feeling to the space. Plus, they're more flexible because one leaf can be locked and the other can remain operable. Also, there are fewer operational and maintenance difficulties.

There are many national, regional, and local window and door companies. From a design standpoint, the larger companies generally offer similar product lines with differences primarily in details, construction methods, finishings, standard sizing, and component aspects.

Doors come in many materials and hundreds of styles, only a few of which are pictured here. You may prefer to use a basic wooden door, a dutch-style door, or antique doors with stained glass inserts.

Screen/Storm Doors & Panels

Although many people prefer a hardy, traditional wooden screen door to the widely available aluminum style, it's a difficult item to find without having the local carpenter build it from scratch. The craft has almost become a lost art form.

There are, however, at least two companies that offer an assortment of styles in standard sizes, as well as custom sizes reminiscent of earlier periods.

One concern is the New England Screen Door Company, which was founded in Bristol, Maine in the late 1980s. Yvonne Hannemann, a New York film producer, went into the business with friend Penny Young after an unsuccessful nationwide search for an acceptable quality wooden model for the porch of Hannemann's summer home.

Employing skills of local craftspeople, the company's collection of eight styles is based on the most common and attractive styles among nearly fifty that the entrepreneurs documented throughout New England. Hannemann says the company tested several kinds of hardwoods and finally settled on South American Cedar as the most durable and sturdy.

The products are air- or kiln-dried to achieve the appropriate moisture content necessary for exterior doors and then finished with a pale gray primer. The pulls are colored ceramic or wood and the spring hinges have adjustable tension.

The doors are made with mortise and tenon joints, and then pegged for additional security. The screen, with an interchangeable storm glass panel, sits in a recessed groove on the back of the door, and is easily secured by clips. In seconds, the door can adapt from summer to winter use. The screen and storm panels are held in place by either brown or white aluminum frames.

Courtesy New England Screen Door Company (all 4 photos on page)

Subtle lighting is best achieved with hidden fixtures. Special effects can be achieved outdoors on stair areas (*above*) and along pathways (*far right*). For glazed areas (*right*), reduce the possibility of the black mirror effect by providing the right kind of illumination.

LIGHTING

Properly planned lighting can visually extend the interior space. And if there are windows, the right illumination can reduce the black mirror effect so you don't see your own reflection at night on the glazed areas.

Like in other rooms, "the most important thing to light is the people" in the space, says Randall Whitehead, president of Light Source, a San Francisco-based lighting consulting firm. Avoid the pitfall of the "museum effect"—the emphasis of accent lighting on plants or art instead of the people in the space. Humanize the room so people are comfortable as well. Besides people, the next priorities to light are the space itself and the objects within the room.

Another aspect to consider are colored temperature lights, which affect how the light source renders color in a room. They can affect illumination, and, having the right color temperature can help keep bugs away. Whitehead suggests tossing out the old notion of buying those little yellow bug lights that theoretically promise to detract flying pests. In fact, the opposite is true. "Bugs are attracted to blue-white lights," Whitehead says. "At the far end of the property we recommend placing a blue-white light, so bugs go to that," instead of to your porch. Use a more traditional color temperature near the house, like regular incandescent bulbs. And if you can, avoid using any yellow bug lights in the porch area. Besides luring bugs, they can camouflage true colors, making the plant life look a bit sickly.

Subtle is Best

Lighting fixtures shouldn't attract attention, and this is particularly important for a porch. "Try to keep the lighting as subtle and as hidden as possible," says Whitehead. For example, choose overhead fixtures the same color as the

© Randy Whitehead/LightSource

Lighting Needs

To determine your lighting needs, visualize how the space will be used in the daytime and in the evenings, and if it'll be weatherized for year-round enjoyment. Considerations include:

- **Dimmer Controls.** Provides the ability to raise or lower the light level depending on the activity.
- **Landscape effects.** Lighting can be balanced or heightened outdoors outside as well, so that the view goes beyond the porch area.
- **Outlets/wiring.** If a concrete slab will be poured for your new porch, think ahead to the number of outlets and mountings required or desired.

Courtesy Gardener's Eden

The proper use of lighting can create a mood and provide comfort, convenience, and safety.

© Randy Whitehead/LightSource

Special lighting effects can be created to provide illumination to the entire exterior of the home (*left*). Other accent lighting includes wall-mounted fixtures (*opposite page, top*). To create special landscaping effects there are a variety of fixtures and light sources available (*opposite page, middle and bottom*).

ceiling and avoid brass or chrome fixtures that can draw too much attention to the lighting system. When these are illuminated, "all you really see is the light bulb inside," says Whitehead. "When ordering fixtures, request sandblasted glass or a white opal glass, so there's the volume of the fixture, instead of just the look of the light bulb inside," he says. The result will be a softer light.

Because the eye always goes to the brightest source of illumination, a light fixture on either side of the door can be distracting when going upstairs or walking along a pathway to the porch area. If you want lighting along the door, "make sure there's a balance of light in the pathway area that's slightly brighter, so it'll guide people towards the porch," Whitehead says.

Moonlighting Effects

For the landscape just outside of the porch, consider other options to lamppost fixtures, which, being bright sources of illumination, attract all the eye's attention.

Whitehead recommends creating a moonlight effect by placing fixtures high in trees, or at their bases; it's a more naturalistic way of lighting the area. "There's a dappled pattern of light and shadow that picks up the branches and throws light down through the leaves to create a pattern on the ground and on any walkway."

Moonlighting apparatus are generically called bullet-shaped fixtures. Most are about nine inches (twenty-two centimeters) long and five inches (twelve centimeters) wide at the mouth of the bullet, and taper to a soft point.

Lighting and Light Fixtures

There are three basic types of lighting you should be familiar with:

General, which provides an area with over-

© Jennifer Levy

Courtesy Toro/Mona Meyer McGrath

Courtesy Williams-Sonoma

all illumination. Your goal should be to create ambient light so people in the space feel comfortable and look good. Fixtures include pendant lights, ceiling or wall-mounted lights, or recessed lights. Indirect lighting is another kind of general illumination; fixtures like wall sconces and torchieres direct diffused light upwards to help avoid glare or shadow caused by direct illumination.

Task, for performing specific activities. The optimum task lighting should be placed between your head and the work surface. In a sitting situation, such as reading, consider a pharmacy-type lamp that comes below eye level so light is thrown onto the book. Do not use recessed or track lights from above for reading.

Accent, for added drama to spotlight or highlight an unusual feature in your decor or landscaping. Recessed or wall-mounted fixtures and low-profile lights for ground and posts can be used for accent light. Another option is track lighting, but only in situations where there isn't enough ceiling depth for recessed fixtures, as track can draw attention to itself. Whitehead suggests that the optimum application is to mount the track on the side of the support beams underneath a tongue-and-groove slanted roof. It can act as a natural baffle for the track so people see what's being lighted.

If the porch will be open to weather elements, make sure that fixtures chosen are properly rated. Damp locations demand fixtures that will withstand dampness and humid conditions. For example, recessed fixtures need to be installed in an eave or an overhang of the porch.

For wall-mounted fixtures that will be relatively open to weather elements, in direct contact with rain or near the ocean, choose fixtures that have been gasketed for a wet location. Specific ratings should be noted in manufacturers' catalogues.

Timers

An automatic timer can control a portion of your outdoor lighting to turn off at a certain hour. Whitehead recommends these systems for an open porch, because it's usually not used on a daily basis. An enclosed porch is a room you'd want to control like any other room in the house.

There are two types of timers—the twenty-four-hour programmable system allows lights to be turned on or off at a certain time each day, and the seven-day programmable timer allows lights to be turned on or off at different times on different days, which is a good security feature.

Light Sources

The performance of any lighting fixture depends on the light source (bulb) used. The degree of energy efficiency and the maintenance required work hand in hand.

Choose bulbs, or lamps as the industry calls them, that have a long life. Whitehead advises against normal household bulbs for exterior fixtures because they have a short life, lasting only about forty-five days.

Instead, he recommends a regular reflector-type bulb like a PAR-38. This parabolic reflector controls light more precisely and produces about four times the light of a household-type bulb. Many of these last for up to 4,500 hours, "so maintenance-wise you don't have to change the bulbs for three to five years."

Another type of light source is low voltage, which reduces energy consumption with more precise beam control. However, these require a transformer. They have a built-in reflector with a halogen bulb for producing superior accent lighting.

Courtesy Four Seasons Greenhouse/ System 6

Today, the fluorescent bulb is an innovative element in lighting design. A compact, or baby fluorescent bulb, called a TL lamp, has been developed. Like a household bulb, fluorescent bulbs used to throw out light equally in all directions. Now, fixtures are made with effective reflectors inside "so the baby fluorescents can throw light out and project it towards trees and plantings," Whitehead says. A 16-watt TL lamp, or baby fluorescent, can give you 75 watts worth of illumination, with a rating of 7,500 hours—ten times the lamp life of a normal household bulb.

The lighting sources you choose can accent both the porch itself and the area surrounding it. Here, the lighting beckons you inside, while the outdoor lighting highlights objects for indoor viewing.

Natural day lighting (*below, top*) can be recreated at night (*below, bottom*) to highlight the environs. Proper lighting can extend the eye visually towards gardens in full bloom.

Another type of light source, much brighter than conventional lamps, is High-Intensity Discharge (HID), which is very energy-efficient and gives tremendous amounts of light for the wattage. One type of HID is mercury vapor, which gives off a blue-green light; another is high-pressure sodium which gives off a pink-orange light.

Whitehead recommends using these sources for lighting a series of post lanterns or along a fence. Another popular HID source is metal halide, a white light that gives a healthy-looking glow to both plants and skin tones.

Color Temperatures

Besides considerations about light sources and fixtures, there are many color temperatures, or degree intervals of color coming from a bulb, that can affect the illumination of your porch and its environs.

Whitehead says the higher the number of degrees, the more blue, white, or green the light will be. Conversely, the lower the number, the more pink-orange the light.

As examples, incandescent household bulbs are 2,800 degrees Kelvin and a cool-light fluorescent is at 5,000 degrees Kelvin. "The incandescent lighting we all grew up with actually is very amber in color and changes our skin color to a more yellow color," Whitehead says. A cool-white fluorescent, on the other hand, is more blue-green.

For warmer color temperatures, choose bulbs that are between 3,000 and 4,000 degrees Kelvin. There's no need to loathe fluorescents any longer—now there are more than 220 colors available.

Even incandescent bulbs are available in different colors. For example, Neolite is the term used for bulbs that are slightly violet in color, which is especially nice for skin tones.

For low-voltage sources, like MR-16 and PAR 36, daylight-blue filters can be purchased. They fit in front of the bulb and reduce the yellow for a bluer-whiter light that is especially good for plants.

To help plan your lighting needs you may want to contact a professional lighting consulting firm. Generally, they require an initial consultation fee and provide a written summary of recommendations. Specification plans, fixtures, and construction costs are additional.

© Randy Whitehead/LightSource

© Randy Whitehead/LightSource

HEATING

There are several heating options to consider if you live in cold-weather climates and want to enjoy your enclosed or convertible porch throughout the year.

Most people heat their homes with traditional systems such as a forced-air furnace, electricity, or hot-water baseboards. Another relatively new alternative is an in-floor system that puts the heating into the floor so that it radiates upward and around with a gentle, even warmth. The in-floor system incorporates improvements in the technology of hydronic radiant heating. Warm water circulates through tubes embedded in a concrete slab or a gypsum-cement underlayment above a suspended floor.

It's a more cost-efficient alternative to other heating systems because the same comfort level can be achieved with a lower thermostat setting, so it's possible to save up to 25 percent on utility bills, according to John Fantauzzi, technical services manager of Gyp-Crete, the Hamel, Minnesota-based company which makes Infloor Heating Systems.

As part of the installation, a thorough design analysis is conducted before the polybutylene tubings or electric cables are fitted underneath the floor. These are then covered with a lightweight, gypsum-based underlayment.

The water that circulates through the tubing can be heated in a boiler, using whatever fuel is most cost-efficient in your area—natural gas, electric, heat pump, wood stove, or solar.

The floor doesn't get uncomfortably hot; the temperature ranges from 70 to 80 degrees Fahrenheit (21 to 27 degrees centigrade).

Under-floor heat performs best with highly conductive floor coverings such as hardwood, tile, or brick. Carpet doesn't work as well because it holds heat to the floor. To allow the heat to radiate more readily through the carpeting, a special bonded urethane pad with low-insulating values is available.

Air-conditioning can work at optimum levels of efficiency and comfort through the heating system. The vents and ducts should be placed high, like the ceiling area, where it can do the most good.

Cozy Stoves

For large enclosed porches that are a part of new home construction, or when converting the type of heating throughout the existing home, there's the option of wood stove heating, or the relatively newer pellet stove for residential use. Both types are for whole-house heating and can be installed as a freestanding unit, or vented on an exterior wall. Some models can be inserted into the fireplace.

The Wood Stove

The wood stove has made a comeback as a popular form of heating in recent years because it now burns much cleaner than the ones available during the boom years of the 1970s when the oil embargo fired their demand.

Today, all wood stoves must meet federal and state clean-air standards. Emission standards set by the Environmental Protection Agency require stoves to carry E.P.A. certification or exemption. Many wood stoves have catalytic converters, which help reduce pollution by recycling and reburning the smoke, making them both cleaner and safer.

The wood stove has not only shed its air-polluter past, but has also lost its unwieldy shape. Designs have undergone a facelift and manufacturers now offer sleeker, more appealing lines. Many have large glass doors in front for optimum fire viewing.

The Pellet Stove

The first pellet stoves for home use were developed in the early 1980s and initially gained popularity in the western United States. They're becoming more widely available across the country as pellet production plants emerge in the Midwest, along the East Coast, and in Canada.

This wood stove (*below*) allows for maximum viewing as well as maximum heating. A wood fire kept burning all day will more than adequately heat up an enclosed porch.

Courtesy Whitfield Pyro Industries Inc.

Pellet stoves are fueled by pencil-shaped, one-and-a-half-inch- (four-centimeter-) long logs made of compressed wood waste. Instead of being loaded into the fire chamber, pellets are placed into a fuel hopper. They can be dispensed automatically to allow a fire to burn for fifty to eighty hours without refueling. Each model has a different burn time and fuel rate, with the lowest being one pound per hour burn rate.

Proper installation of both types of stove is a must. Dealers have installation professionals or will recommend independent contractors. And check with your local buildings department or fire department about safety codes.

Courtesy Nutone (both photos)

VENTILATION

While in some cases windows and doors provide sufficient airflow to enclosed porches, other situations may require air-conditioning or a home ventilating system to remove hot, stuffy air in minutes.

Small ventilation systems are especially important for areas with a lot of glass so air intake and exhaust can be controlled by the thermostat. Also, for an area like a whirlpool, there are special fan products to control the temperature and moisture.

Whenever the outside temperature is below 82 degrees F (28 degrees C), a ventilation system works by moving air and evaporating moisture from skin and clothing, thereby reducing body temperature.

In many areas such a system will eliminate the need for air-conditioning. In high temperature and humid areas where air-conditioning is a necessity, a home ventilation system can reduce air-conditioning operation costs.

A ventilation system brings the cool outdoors inside. For example, in the early evening hours, open screened windows about twelve inches (thirty centimeters) in the porch area. Turn the fan inside the system on high speed, and it will cool the air throughout the ventilated area. To further balance the system, dial the solid state control to the desired level of ventilation.

The system can be easily installed through a wall, roof, or ceiling and features a solid-state air volume control and automatic night shut-off timer. It can cool up to four rooms at the same time. Decorative wall/ceiling grilles have a built-in, close-off damper.

If you have an enclosed porch it is important to have some type of heating and ventilation system. Two different systems are shown here (*left and above*). Ceiling fans (*opposite page*) effectively circulate the air in both open and closed porches. They are also a beautiful design accessory.

© Allan Weitz

Ceiling Fans

Another way of cooling off your porch is with a ceiling paddle fan, which draws in fresh air. It can mix and circulate the air evenly and works especially well with air-conditioning and in rooms with high ceilings.

There are a variety of blade sizes and styling choices available from ornate to clean and contemporary. Finishes include polished or antique brass, wood grains, and solid colors in basic or fashion hues.

Many ceiling fans are also available with lights. Interchangeable light kits from a single light to five-light clusters can be operated by a pull-chain switch, or controlled by a wall switch.

Air flow is reversible for year-round comfort and energy savings. Direct it down in summer to feel cooler, and up in winter to de-stratify air at the ceiling.

Some models come with a computerized wall control for total fan and light command, plus preprogrammed convenience and security features. For example, the fan and/or the light can be scheduled to turn on or off after a specified period.

© Rion Rizzo Creative Sources Photography Inc.

Porch Presence

Columns, capitals, and bases add character and flair to traditional porches. Whether standing alone or paired with balustrades, these design elements can be finished to match the exterior trim.

© Sandra Dos Passos

BALUSTRADES, COLUMNS, & LATTICES

Any number of closely spaced symmetrical supports can make up a balustrade or railing. Called balusters or spindles, these rounded wood braces can be tapered at each end or swell towards the top and bottom. Teamed with finely carved columns or posts, these architectural details exude refined function.

Stately columns made of wood or aluminum won't rot or split with age. Those with a factory-applied primed finish make them ready for painting to match exterior trim.

Authentically detailed capitals and bases are proportioned for each column, and offered in varying diameters and lengths. Besides standard applications, columns also lend themselves to special installations, such as easy placement around existing supports (with split caps and bases), conversions to half and three-

© Donn Young

First came wood; in recent years PVC has become widely used for improved durability. Wood or PVC lattice-work provide design appeal for foundation areas, walls, stair railings, and even arbors.

quarter columns mounted against walls and corners, and modification to provide intermediate support for a second-story porch.

Most decorative railings and spindles are made of pressure-treated wood and come in a variety of classic and contemporary styles.

Lattice is another design element that adds charm to a porch. These panel treatments are popular as traditional porch and stair railings, arbors, screen walls, and screen underpinnings for foundations.

For years these slats were made of wood and then painted to match the decor. Now there's an alternative to wood that provides better durability and easier installation and maintenance: polyvinyl chloride (PVC) lattice.

The panels are fabricated from reinforced polyester strips in which the joints are chemically welded together rather than stapled, glued, or nailed. There's no need to paint because the panels are offered in a variety of standard colors as well as custom tints. Cross Industries, Inc., Atlanta, Georgia, is a leading maker with its VINYLattice. Panels are offered in two patterns: diagonal and rectangular. Each pattern is available in three types, varying by strip width and hole opening size.

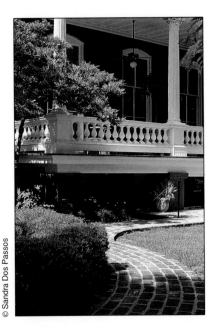

© Sandra Dos Passos

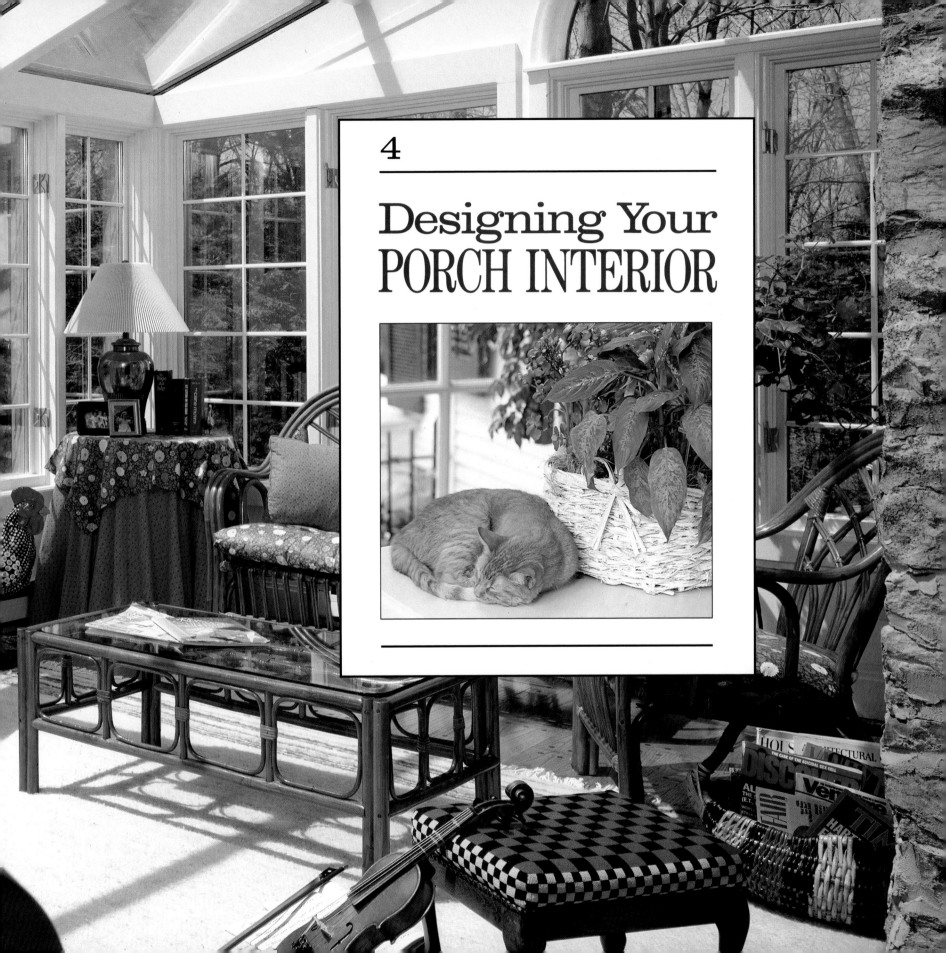

4

Designing Your
PORCH INTERIOR

MATERIALS FOR PORCH INTERIORS

Creating a personality for your porch decor begins with the basic layout of the space and the selection of materials and furnishings for decorating it. Determine the overall mood you want to project: open and outdoorsy, bright and cheery, or warm and intimate. "Generally, porches call for a more relaxed style of living, so choices should reflect it," says interior designer Peter F. Carlson.

© Jeff McNamara

Core schematic materials are paint, flooring, window treatment, decorative fabric, and wall covering, if the space will be fully enclosed.

You may want to key the color scheme to an adjoining room or to favorite furniture or to upholstered cushions and decorative treatments you plan to use.

© Bill Rothschild/ design by Marilyn Rose

PAINT

There are several kinds of paint and many are suited to a particular surface. The basic choices are solvent-thinned alkyd- and oil-based paints, which are durable and resist abrasion well, or water-thinned latex paints, which are also long-wearing, easy to apply, and retain color well. Latex paints are often more popular because they clean up easily with just soap and water.

Either alkyd or latex types can be used successfully, provided the surface is properly prepared. Whichever you choose, determine the quality of paint by the percentage of binders, or resins, and the pigment. The higher the percentage of pigment and binders, the better the paint, according to David G. Frye, Sherwin-Williams, Sayville, New York.

Although paint labels list the content, the proportions of binders and pigments are no longer indicated by makers. Ask your local retailer/distributor about the ratio of pigment, which gives paint its color and hiding power, and binders, which allow the mixture to adhere. The higher the content of binders and pigments the easier and better the paint will cover the surface.

Most major paint companies guarantee their paints for a number of years. A longer guarantee, higher price, and quality go hand in hand.

Paint life is difficult to predict because there are a number of factors involving the underlay and the weather conditions in exterior paint situations. When choosing a paint consider national brands over lesser-known labels, but keep in mind that the larger companies have many levels of quality in their lines.

Determine Gloss

For alkyd (oil) and latex paints you can choose from several kinds of glosses, or degrees of shine. The standard are flat, semi-gloss, and gloss. The finer the pigment is ground the shinier the gloss. Variations can include dead flat, regular flat, eggshell (also called satin or velvet), semigloss, and high-gloss. Every paint brand offers different degrees of shine.

For most surfaces, the shinier the paint the more durable its performance. Also, glossier paints are easier to wash. Unlike flat paints, the shinier ones are harder to touch up.

For ceilings, which are usually imperfect surfaces, it's advisable to use a flat paint because fewer blemishes will show through.

Enamels, available in latex or alkyd, are popular for covering wood flooring because they're so durable, especially for highly tracked surfaces. They provide hardness and shine and are available in high or low gloss.

© Ken Murphy/C. F. Weber Photography

Most porch owners pay special attention to making their porch compatible with the rest of the home. There are so many colors and stains available that you may have to test many colors until you find those right for you.

Paint Colors

When choosing exterior colors for the porch, consider the color of neighboring homes so your choice will be compatible. Your region or style of home may sway your decision. If the porch is being restored to historical preservation standards, contact the local society for direction. When adding or renovating a porch, determine the color that goes best with the body and trim colors of your home. "Generally, people paint their [exterior] porch the same color as the house trim, but that's not a rule that has to be followed," says Frye.

Pastels are popular and are often coordinated with darker accent tones. Also, reproduction colors from the eighteenth and nineteenth centuries, like shades of red, blue, yellow, and green, have been making a comeback for Colonial, Federal, and Victorian style homes.

When choosing an overall color, consider the amount of sunlight the porch will receive. A highly lit space won't make a dark color look drab. Be careful, because darker base colors may fade or appear to have faded more often than lighter tones.

If you will be painting the wooden flooring, consider a shade of gray or another light hue because these are less likely to show dust and track marks than darker colors.

Stains and Finishes

Exterior wood stains are popular for textured wood surfaces. Solid stains hide the color of the wood, but allow the texture to show through; if you want a more natural wood color, choose semi-transparent stains.

In other coatings, it is not advisable to put clear polyurethanes on wood, particularly if the porch is open to weather elements. Unlike regular varnishes, these don't hold up as well under direct sunlight. Also, polyurethanes can turn white when in contact with water. A better alternative is an oil-based varnish or stain that penetrates well. The wood shouldn't be fresh or extremely dried out before applying the stain.

If your porch is already covered in an oil-based stain, you can use a latex product on top of it because the wood has already been sealed.

Another option to consider is a bleaching stain which gives the look of uniform, naturally weathered wood.

© William B. Seitz

Courtesy Western Wood Products Association

Courtesy Western Wood Products Association

Color Tricks

Depending upon your decorating demands, there are color styling tricks to consider:

- Contrast colors to emphasize architectural features, such as moldings. Paint them a darker or lighter color than the walls.

© Donn Young

- Create interest where there's none; in a square, enclosed porch, paint one wall an accent color.
- Unify the exterior of a home made with different materials, such as brick and wood, by using the same color or a slightly different shade.
- Use a dark color on a too-high ceiling to make it appear lower.
- Modify the proportions of a long, narrow porch and make it seem wider by painting the shorter walls a darker color than the longer walls.

Courtesy Western Wood Products Association

FLOOR COVERINGS

In step with fashion, flooring products today offer countless species: wood can be treated to many looks, and resilient and non-resilient floorings are available in every style, color, texture, and faux finish (finishes that imitate an actual finish such as marble) imaginable. For extra decorative touches, place area rugs atop ceramic tile, dimension stone, vinyl, and wood for color oomph and pattern intrigue.

The selection process involved in choosing flooring can be confusing. Begin by putting practicality underfoot—select flooring that's best suited for how open or enclosed the space

will be to the weather elements. Wood, ceramic tile, and dimension stone are recommended materials for open and semi-open porches. If you fancy outdoor carpeting, there are a few innovative fiber options that have outclassed artificial turfs.

Wood

In sawn lumber, there are many species of hard and soft woods, many indigenous to specific regions. Western woods, for example, include Douglas Fir, Hem-Fir, Engelman Spruce, Idaho White Pine, Western Cedars, and Incense Cedar. Cypress and Yellow Poplar are among Eastern natives, as is Southern Pine, which is pressure-treated with chemical preservatives that penetrate deeply into the cellular structure. If properly treated, this wood resists decay and termites.

Waterborne preservatives are most commonly used on woods for home construction because of their clean appearance. They also meet stringent E.P.A. health guidelines. Wood treated with this preservative can be stained or painted when dry.

Redwoods are popular for outdoor rooms, too, and there are several grades that range from those textured with knots to others free or nearly free of knots. Exterior finishes such as water repellents, stains, and bleaching oils can enhance Redwood's natural weathering ability, according to the California Redwood Association, Novato, California.

Selecting the right hard or soft wood is a matter of preference and pocketbook. In hard woods, for example, oak is quite expensive, while yellow poplar is inexpensive. To help skim costs, consider thinner boards; a two-by-four size instead of two-by-six, for example.

Besides plank and strip flooring, other popular configurations are diagonal, square, herringbone, and parquet patterns.

The options available in floor coverings are nearly endless. A few of the possibilities are displayed here (*left*): choose wood flooring that is stained or bleached; top wood floors with beautiful oriental rugs; clay, ceramic, or vinyl tiles all hold up especially well in open porches; carpet comes in many lengths, colors, and materials. The key to choosing a floor covering is in determining the kind of wear it will get and whether or not it will be exposed to the elements.

Wood is popular for all kinds of porches, open or closed. Choose from countless species and looks that vary depending upon how you stain and finish them.

Vinyl tiles come in many different styles, including simulated wood (*right*). Both vinyl and terra cotta (*below*) are wonderful floor coverings for open or enclosed porches. They hold up under adverse weather conditions and heavy traffic; they are easy to care for and when topped with area rugs, take on an entirely new look.

Stains and Finishes

There are striking effects that can be created with stains and finishes. For example, give the floor a pale, streaked look with pickling or bleaching techniques. For a country look, apply stencil designs as a simple overall or border pattern in tones that coordinate with the color scheme. You can have a local artist customize a pattern, purchase a design at a decorating center, or create your own, using materials from art supply stores. Another country look is a painted-on "floorcloth" in faded shades on the naturally finished floor.

Courtesy Azrock Floor Products

Courtesy USG Interiors

Ceramic Tile

It's difficult to match the inherent properties of ceramic tile for durability, decorative impact, and low-maintenance. Also, tile's conductive quality makes it a natural for porch floors as well as walls.

Tile-clad concrete surfaces act as thermal masses; they absorb, store, and slowly release the sun's heat in winter. In the summer, tiles absorb cool breezes.

When choosing tile, pick one that has a mat or textured finish, or is commercially rated and frost-resistant for exterior applications.

Unglazed quarry tile is generally used on floors and in outdoor areas because it is more durable and scratch-resistant than glazed tile, according to the Tile Council of America, Princeton, New Jersey. And, unglazed tile maintains its natural clay color and develops a gloss as it ages.

Pale neutral and bold primary colors are among the wide range of hues available for tiles. Pair solid colors and set them diagonally or in a checkerboard fashion. Combine patterns with solids. Tiles are also made in more textural qualities in faux finishes such as leather, wood grains, marble, and granite.

The grout you choose is just as important as the tile. There are many colors to fill the spaces between the tile; coordinate with or contrast the tile color.

Cushiony Underfoot

Also recommended for fully enclosed porches is vinyl flooring, which comes in tile form or sheets (usually in big rolls). The category these two fall in is called resilient flooring because of the bit of give for extra comfort unlike hard surface materials.

Resilients are not intended to stand up to outdoor wear because adhesives don't bond during cold weather and the grouting/seams aren't water-tight.

In vinyl tiles, the best value comes with solid vinyl, as it is the most durable. Vinyl composition tile is less expensive because it contains a combination of vinyl and other materials.

To get the best perspective of vinyl tiles available, shop at a large floor covering dealer that's likely to carry an enormous range of patterns, textures, and colors.

Some patterns mimic marble, slate with mortar brick, granite, ceramic and quarry tile,

Courtesy Azrock Floor Products

Above: **This beautiful floor is an elegant addition to any porch.**

and brick in herringbone designs. Also, there are wood grains that stand alone as plank, stripping, and parquet styles, plus some with bleached color finishes, or a mix of wood with brick mortar effects.

There are custom vinyl tiles, too, in richly colored leather tones, calfskins, small prints, polka dots, checks, cork, and pearl looks, and many kinds of surface textures and bevels from slate to lizard.

If you prefer vinyl sheet floors, (the successors to linoleum since the 1970s), there are also a myriad of patterns and textures, plus the advantage of few seams. It usually comes in six- or twelve-feet (two- or four-meter) wide rolls. There are many grades and price ranges available.

The top category in vinyl sheet flooring is inlaid vinyl. These designs undergo a styling process that builds up layers of vinyl granules that are fused under heat and pressure. The result is a deep, rich color. Their sturdy construction makes them more resistant to tearing and puncturing. The other major category is rotovinyl; designs are imprinted on the surface and protected by a clear top layer. The backing is a foam cushioning for extra resilience.

Dimension Stone

Stones like marble, granite, and slate are called dimension stones because they have been quarried and squared to a specified length, width, and thickness in slab or tile form.

Although some people may think of these stones as decorating luxuries, they're more readily available today and, consequently, more competitive in price. In fact, some marble tiles are less expensive than high-end ceramic tiles.

In granite, the palette extends from whites to blacks. For slate there are tones of black, gray, blue, green, and red. Marble comes in nearly any shade imaginable. Each type of

stone offers many finishes. Choose a textured finish that has been honed to assure better slip-resistance when wet.

Enclosed Flooring Choices

Fully enclosed porches can be dressed with most any kind of floor covering, from the natural hard surfaces—wood, tile, stone—to sisal and coir natural fiber matting and vinyl flooring that comes in tile form or wide roll sheets.

Sisal and coir are popular woven materials because of their practicality and attractiveness as mattings. Sisal is made of yarns spun from the sisal fibers extracted from the long spike-shaped leaves of the tropical sisal plant. Hand-spun coir yarns are pulled from the tough, fibrous husks that surround the coconut.

Like other yarns made of vegetable fibers, both sisal and coir have natural variations in size, shade, and tendency to return to their original color after exposure to sunlight. They're durable, too; traffic patterns don't show even after constant use. These mattings are available in a variety of textures and colors, plus offer thermal and acoustical qualities.

Experts say these mattings are best for enclosed areas because sisal shrinks and coir expands, then slightly contracts when wet.

Both types can be installed wall-to-wall over a firm pad using tack-strip, in a similar manner as conventional carpeting. This method is often preferred over glue-down, as it allows a softer feel underfoot, and does not alter the original floor surface. Also available are mattings with latex backing that reduce the amount of stretch and minimize the raveling of cut edges during installation. This type of backing is suggested for high-traffic areas.

If your home is located in a region with great fluctuations in humidity or temperature, it's not advisable to loose-lay these mattings because they may wrinkle in these conditions.

For enclosed porches, flooring can set the color scheme. Here, terra cotta tiles complement the natural wood flooring of the adjacent deck and add a warm feeling to this space. The rich color is enhanced with area rugs and white rattan furniture upholstered in complementary fabrics.

WALL COVERINGS

Wall coverings help set the mood and can even help solve spatial dilemmas in your porch.

Vinyls and synthetics are among the broad array of wall coverings available. There are also engaging looks, textures, and colors in ceramic tiles, as well as natural vegetable fiber imports like sisal and coir matting, which have thermal qualities. An entirely different effect can be created with wood paneling.

In the vinyl category, there are prepasted, vinyl-coated materials having a dry adhesive backing that's applied wet. Also, choose among solid vinyl materials that are not pre-pasted; their backings are paper, cheesecloth, or synthetic. Because of a thicker vinyl face and substantial backing, solid vinyls are especially good to cover minor surface imperfections. They're scrubbable, too.

The style options range from elegant, hand-printed designs to grass cloth materials, brick, watered silk effects, bright, bold patterns, and soft neutrals.

When selecting a pattern or coordinates of wall coverings and/or fabrics designed to correlate, there's no rule-of-thumb for enclosed porches. Like any other space, choose whatever the style dictates—Victorian, country, traditional, or neoclassical. Use stenciling motifs for countrified special effects, or mural wall coverings on one wall to enhance the feeling of the outdoors.

You may want to play a pattern against a solid, or coordinate the colors of wall coverings and fabrics. For example, use floral coordinates for the walls, window treatments, and tablecloth, and strategic repeats in little touches like a throw pillow on a chair covered in a color-coordinated solid fabric.

Vinyl and synthetic wall coverings can solve visually tricky problems. If, for example, the ceiling is low, choose patterns with a definite upward thrust, like a trellis motif. Add to the illusion with light-colored and airy designs on the ceiling. Optically lower high ceilings with a dark-toned wall covering; the addition of a wide border motif on a solid colored wall creates a cozy effect.

Small spaces can be perceptually "stretched" by use of small or open patterns—trelliswork, louvered shutters, or fretwork—in light colors. Reverse the illusion in large or extra-long spaces with richly colored wall coverings so the space feels warmer.

Below: **This floral-patterned wall covering is nicely complemented by the chair's upholstery and cushions.**

Courtesy J. Josephson, Inc.

Wood Paneling

Pattern and texture are hallmarks of wood paneling. For example, wood boards can be installed vertically, so rooms with lower ceilings seem taller. Likewise, horizontal applications tend to de-emphasize height, forcing the perception of width. Solid boards can be laid in a variety of patterns. For a seamless, contemporary look there's interlocking tongue-and-groove edges. A more pronounced visual effect can be created by overlapping edges.

Wood's tonal feel spans the spectrum from the genteel glazed finish to the warmth of rough-sawn, natural boards. It can form a tangible link with outdoor elements and, in effect, bring the outside in. And with an expanse of glass or stone, accenting touches of wood lend a warming complement.

A wood-clad wall is compatible with any finish you may want to use, but there are technical properties worth inquiring about. Among the options are glazes, which can be painted and wiped, wet-rubbed, or dry-sanded to reveal subtle wood tones. Lighten the wood by bleaching. Use varnish that can be tinted with pigmented universal stainers or artist oil colors. For transparent looks, there are water-soluble dyes and polyurethane varnishes.

Several words of caution about rough, natural wood. Harsh, direct light will throw any surface texture into shadowy relief, deepening the color value of the wall. Also, if wood is sealed and stained, it will invariably darken with age. The combination of these effects can make a room seem decidedly smaller. Available as a guide to wood paneling is "Interiors Workbook," offered by the Western Wood Products Association, Yeon Building, 522 SW Fifth Ave., Portland, OR 97204-2122.

Rely on your interior designer, or the local decorating center or home center for expert advice when purchasing wall coverings.

Courtesy Georgia-Pacific (both photos on page)

Wood paneling provides a rustic look to any porch. To ensure that your paneling will last for years, be sure to seal it.

WINDOW TREATMENTS & DECORATIVE FABRICS

© Peter Paige Assoc./ design by E. Lewis

© Phillip H. Ennis

On the one hand, by its very nature, the porch's relaxing, alfresco presence is incongruous with window treatments and fabric effects as part of the cozy decor. And yet, there is validity in softening particularly large exterior rooms with fabrics that add color and texture. However, some applications are more practical than others.

Architect Kenneth Narza, of Planned Expansion Group, North White Plains, New York, contends that when windows are properly framed within the composition, the addition of window treatments is a fairly arbitrary element. Shutters, however, are part of the architectural design, not decoration. "A house with a porch tends to be irregular in shape and there's no reason, or easy way, to build in a pocket for storing draperies," he says. And when there's floor-to-ceiling glass, the lines are pure and clean; the addition of draperies would only diminish that openness.

Put your subjectivity to work, particularly with an open porch. Decide if you prefer low-maintenance options over more opulent, non-weatherized fabric treatments that may have to be replaced after a season's use. Designer Josef Pricci, New York, is an arbiter of bringing decorative fabrics into play providing a feeling of comfort and luxury so the porch is "as elaborate as the drawing room."

Larger porches, like a wraparound veranda, are more conducive to special fabric effects than small spaces, says Pricci. For example, for an open porch with a series of posts, treat the space between them as walls whether they're

Tented ceilings (*above left*) and balloon treatments for the windows (*above*) can nicely soften an open or an enclosed porch and add color and texture.

glazed or unglazed. Install floor-to-ceiling pinch-pleated draperies and tie them back with a decorative cord. They can conceal the columns and invite a bit of privacy.

Another open-air treatment is to create a tentlike ceiling with fabric. Besides softening the space, the effect plays up the outdoors.

For smaller porches, treat the posts as window frames; install a textured blind between them and top with a fabric-covered valance.

Another choice for open porches is the balloon shade, although it's a bit impractical. Humidity and moisture buildup will make replacement required after each season. To lend some protection, roll-up panels of lucid plastic can be installed behind the shades.

Weatherization should be a consideration when choosing fabrics. Cottons are fine, but avoid fabrics woven from yarns that can shrink, like linen, when exposed to humidity.

There's a spectrum of window treatments for enclosed porches, ranging from various kinds of shades to swags and festoons.

Fully glazed porches, or sunspaces, may not need any fabric dressing at all. Special glass options in climate control window systems fine-tune comfort. Optional blinds and pleated shades, below sloped roof glass and between panes of windows and doors, help regulate energy, shade, and privacy.

Awnings

Fabric awnings and panels are obvious choices for porches. Functionally, they are great protectors from sun and rain. They're decorative, too, and can dress up porch areas and windows, or give them a more casual appeal. Choose awnings that reflect the architecture of your home, or give fresh life to a rather ordinary facade.

Most awnings are custom-made and are available in six generic fabrics: acrylic painted

© Steven Brooke

army duck; acrylic coated cotton; vinyl coated cotton; vinyl laminated polyester; solution-dyed acrylic; and coated polyester. These fabric types have undergone rigorous testing for weathering, durability, flame-retardancy, and other performance characteristics, according to The Awning Division of Industrial Fabrics Association International, St. Paul, Minnesota. Most are water-repellent or waterproof. Choose from an array of solid colors—brilliants, classics, and pastels—and a variety of stripes and multi-patterns. Styles include retractable and standard stationary.

There are a number of metal materials used for framework systems. The manufacturer can help you decide which is best for your needs, based upon your preference and regional variations such as codes and climatic conditions.

Besides providing protection and decoration, awnings conserve energy by shading glazed areas and reducing the interior temperature. The exact amount of heat reduction depends upon the exposure, fabric color, style, and method of attachment.

Above: Awnings add color and provide shade for your porch. They also help protect furniture from the elements. Most awnings can be rolled up to let the sun shine in.

FURNITURE & ACCOUTREMENTS

Beyond the nostalgic Adirondack chair, antique wicker, and the proverbial wooden swing there are scores of high-spirited casual furniture styles for outfitting the porch. Choose from a variety of frame constructions, seatings, and decorative pieces to fit classic, traditional, or contemporary styles. Whatever you fancy, particularly for porches open to the elements, select furnishings that are weatherized.

Many materials are offered in a variety of pieces to suit your needs. Sofas and loveseats, some of which come with gliders; steamer chairs, rockers, and loungers; beds, benches, ottomans, and settees; tables and chairs for dining; or side tables, trunks, and coffee tables.

Many outdoor, casual furniture framing styles today are made of aluminum because it's a durable, rust-proof material that's also unaffected by ultraviolet light.

In tubular and extruded aluminum, look for brands that use thick, heavy-gauge alloys that are coated with a hard, durable finish. There's a colorful palette to choose from. Designs are shaped into many beautiful "arms and legs" such as triangle tubing, Art Deco, free-flowing shapes, and drawn aluminum in single or multiple tubing for fluted and wide or flat frames.

Among the seating choices are straps made of vinyl lacing, which can be used alone or topped with cushions. Look for vinyl straps that have been treated with mildew inhibitors and ultraviolet stabilizers for the best retention and color-wear qualities.

Slings are another seating choice for tubular aluminum frames. Light and airy looking, slings are made of vinyl-coated polyester fiber materials and provide a sturdy and comfortable suspension surface.

A more elegant, intricately formed design style is cast aluminum furniture. Each original

© E. A. McGee/FPG International

part is hand-carved in wood. These parts become the pattern for the metal plate which is used to make the final, solid aluminum castings; they are later assembled and finished by hand. Extremely strong and virtually rust-free, cast aluminum offers a range of beautifully detailed adaptations in a variety of classic, clean lines or more baroque in appeal. Some designs are finished in a rich, antique verdigris.

For more casual comfort and style there's wicker, with an updated life style benefit—all-weather construction. Lloyd/Flanders, Menominee, Michigan, offers a unique series of wicker furniture that's formed onto sturdy aluminum frames. The baked-on polyester finish eliminates cracking, peeling, and burrs, which are typical longevity problems of most other wicker products that should only be used indoors.

This painted wood furniture (*opposite page*) is both elegant and rugged—perfect for porching. In this enclosed porch (*above*), upholstered couches combine with wood and glass tables and rattan furniture.

95

Rattan is fresh and traditional fare for porching (*below*). Another classic, more formal furniture material is wrought iron (*right*), made of heavy gauge rolled steel.

The company has combined new technology and designs using Lloyd Looms, the patented weaving process created in the early nineteenth century. Available in an array of colors, styles are either reminiscent of original Lloyd Loom furniture found in antique stores today, or they're more oversized and contemporary.

The famous Lloyd Loom wicker baby carriages, circa 1920s, are also reproduced, but only for decorative uses like a serving cart or plant stand.

Courtesy Winterthur

In wrought-iron frames, which are made of heavy gauge, high-carbon rolled steel, there's a whole different flair of classic, casual outdoor furniture. Styling can be lattice/grid patterns, simple flowing lines, old-fashioned refinement, veranda-like designs, or even more ornate.

Frame parts are shaped by automatic presses with specially designed dies. The best quality wrought-iron frames are handground for a smooth appearance. There are many rich paint finishes, from antique blue to cinnabar, that are abrasion- and weather-resistant.

A holdout from the 1950s, the classic American outdoor seat, the "lawn" chair, has been recaptured and updated. Constructed of heavy gauge steel, the chairs tout contoured seats, rounded arms, and now flaunt aluminum tubular framing. They're sturdier than ever and the baked-on finish offers a rainbow of colors.

Handsome wood species—redwood, teak, mahogany, and cherry among them—provide another approach to decking the porch in traditional or contemporary fare. Depending on the wood, they are sometimes finished or painted to withstand weather elements.

Teak, in particular, has become more widely available in the United States. Even within the classic styles, the quality of construction and furniture weight can vary greatly. Because the lighter the furniture the less costly it's apt to be, compare weights as well as prices.

© Phillip H. Ennis

© Jeff McNamara

Woods can clothe your porch in untold styles including English adaptations, classics, and vernacular modes, like the Tennessee rocking chair. For rustic flavor there are many inspirations, too. For example, handcrafted cherry furniture with a Mayan influence and folding chairs without nails, screws, or bolts. Or craftsmanship in traditional Mexican style; the Equipales chair made of natural pigskin, willow reed, and cedar battens. Any of these styles can be spiced with brightly colored pillows.

Very different from wood, metal, or plastic is synthetic resin furniture. It's finished in lacquer and has an avant-garde charm in traditional and modern shapes. The material is completely unaffected by temperature extremes and retains its shape, suppleness, and comfort with no discoloration or cracking. Metal parts are made of aluminum or stainless steel to withstand the toughest atmospheric conditions.

Besides a full line of furniture pieces for the outdoors, some synthetic resin makers offer space-saving features. For example, convertible tables built with two sets of legs, so the height can be adapted for your purposes.

Wood can easily dress a porch in countless styles, including this rustic, casual look (*above*). **It can be made more formal with colorful cushions and a matching table cloth.**

UPHOLSTERY

Crisp, colored fabrics for cushions and throw pillows are cheery decorative touches that can spring your outdoor living room into full bloom. Stripes, florals, or solids are popular choices. And when colors are compatible, don't be timid about mixing and matching the patterns.

In the past, vinyl-coated polyester has always been the leading fabric for upholstery exposed to weather elements; today it continues to be a good choice, available in several constructions including jacquard and basket weave.

Another preference is an acrylic fabric in jacquard weaves, solids, and a variety of patterns as well. Cottons, chintzes, and canvases are also available and many are treated to resist dirt and stains.

© Jennifer Levy

© Phillip H. Ennis

For an easy decorative change, cover sofa seat cushions with a traditional quilt, complemented by solid color throw pillows for a more provincial mood. Or, when fall breezes begin to blow, wrap the cushions with woolen blankets in primary colors and stripes.

Most cushions are filled with polyester, and there are varying degrees of quality. Others are made of muslin-encased foam and fiberfill. Some fills hold their loft while others flatten out in a few weeks. Check to see if they are waterproof; if cushions and pillows are mildew-resistant only, and they will be outdoors, they should be stored inside when there's rain or humidity. For upholstery that will withstand a lot of moisture, select a foam stuffing that allows water to drain thoroughly.

Cotton, chintz, and canvas are popular upholstery fabrics. Accent these fabrics with decorative pillows in coordinating colors and patterns. The fabrics you choose can say a lot about you and help dictate the look of the porch.

TABLES & TOPS

Tables, whether for dining or occasional use, should be functional, long-lasting, and aesthetically pleasing. Surface materials can match the body, like wood, wicker, and synthetic resins. Many tables geared for outdoor wear are designed with transparent tops because they're airy, durable, and easy to clean. Options include tempered smooth-rough glass, acrylic for a more textured look, and clear solar glass. Also, beveled glass edges can add a nice finishing touch.

Add a glass top or a granite surface to an existing tabletop. Or, if your decor is eclectic with an ornate flair, consider using Corinthian columns and pedestals topped with cut-to-fit glass or stone in rounded shapes as side tables or for dining.

© Jeff McNamara

Tabletops for munching can be creative, makeshift spreads. Top a wicker trunk with a piece of finished wood (*left*) to create a table. For a side table, top a Corinthian pedestal with a cut-to-fit piece of glass or plexiglass (*below*).

Courtesy Williams-Sonoma

Alfresco dining can be made more luxurious when the table is dressed up with a custom-made tablecloth and matching seat cushions.

Entertaining large groups usually requires a contingency plan for extra dining space. Don't despair about using those old metal card tables and folding chairs; ready their party clothes! Foldaway, vinyl-covered fiberboards in round shapes can be set up easily over card tables and draped in pretty fabric tablecloths. Add chair covers made of cotton or poly/cotton in coordinating fabric and voilà—dressings for a more elegant and comfier feast.

Made of fiberglass-reinforced plaster of paris, these columns are decorative and sturdy and come in various sizes. For example, a ten-and-a-half inch (twenty-five centimeter) diameter base standing sixteen inches (thirty-eight centimeters) high is suitable as a side table. A taller, pedestal size can be crowned by a lavish bouquet of flowers.

ACCOUTREMENTS

Accessories are pivotal style-clinchers that can impart convenience and enjoyment to porching activities, or simply give decorative élan.

Multifunctional gear is especially germane to porches. Carts, for instance, can be practical choices for entertaining as well as a helpmate for gardening chores. One dual-purpose model is a solid, weather-resistant mahogany and stained redwood cart that's a great accessory for barbecue and serving refreshments, or use it as a potting bench. When the lid of the tray area is uncovered, the receptable can be a handy catchall for gardening paraphernalia.

Your potting table can easily double as a table bar by adding a fabric skirt.

Whether you have a flower garden or not, add a dose of greenery for color and warm appeal. Decorative planters, troughs, window boxes, or flowerpots filled with lush foliage, plants, herbs, or freshly cut petals add a splash of color to any porch.

Planters and window boxes come in many woods, including teak, cedar, and cypress, as well as copper. Put plant stands in a grouping. Some are stackable, while others are designed to fit snugly over railings and around corners. Marry classical styling with the best of modern materials. Fiberglass planter boxes mimic the fielded panels of traditional wooden planter boxes, yet will not decay and need no painting. Add an obelisk form that's tailored to fit on large planters to train ivy and other evergreen vines into a pyramid shape.

Wooden troughs can be more than extra large planters. Use them to border the room; some are big enough to contain a hedge. Both big and small hand-molded terra-cotta planters and pots are a rich touch, too. For herbs and low, sprawling plants there are square-rimmed and oval pots plus rimmed pots sized to fit hand-forged iron trivets. Some terra-cotta pots

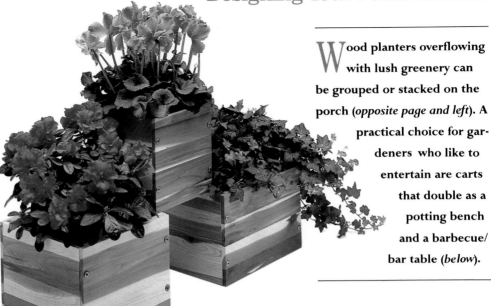

Wood planters overflowing with lush greenery can be grouped or stacked on the porch (*opposite page and left*). A practical choice for gardeners who like to entertain are carts that double as a potting bench and a barbecue/bar table (*below*).

Courtesy Ringer Co. (both photos)

incorporate a simple yet ingenious water reservoir system that keeps soil and pot walls moist for days or weeks.

Some plant stands combine form with function. For instance, a wrought-iron table with a clear glass top features a shelf area underneath for showing off flowering plants or potted herbs. If you adore big, informal flower arrangements, there's the fresh appeal of French florist buckets made of galvanized steel with tall, tapered sides, welded handles, and banded bottoms.

© William B. Seitz

You may not want to encumber the porch with too many accessories, but some decorative touches to consider are inexpensive prints in botanical motifs to hang on the wall, or a dried, scented wreath. An antique wood bird cage is also a good accent piece, whether placed on a pedestal stand or on a table. If there aren't windows on the abutting structure of the porch, have a local artisan create a backdrop painting on stretched canvas, like a surrealistic portrait of flowers and greenery in pigments apropos to your decorating scheme.

Woven baskets, in many shapes and sizes, can add texture and color, too. On the floor they can contain dried flowers with a brightly colored cotton square neatly tied along the handle, or tucked inside. Heap exotic fruits in a reed basket, or, if your porch is seaside or near the swimming pool, stuff it with lush, rolled towels.

Woven baskets in all shapes and sizes are practical and decorative accessories for porch wear. Fill with fresh or dried flowers for color (*far left*). This Japanese-inspired porch (*left*) is simple, yet elegant and comfortable. Throw pillows on the benches and ground add comfort and a splash of color, while the potted flowers add color and beauty.

Courtesy California Redwood Association/photo: © Ernest Braun

105

Courtesy Weber Stephen Products

The worry-free Genesis gas grill from Weber (*left*) with its flavorizer system allows the barbecue flavor to go back into the food; there are no hot or cold spots and no charring. The style of your porch can help define how you use it. A porch like this one (*right*) with both open and closed areas allow you to fully enjoy the art of porching. *Far right:* One of the hi-tech options available for porching is this combination radio-cassette/intercom.

For entertaining, you may like to barbecue but loathe the traditional, and often messy routine of charcoal grilling, or are cautious about the additional safety hazards of gas grilling. A more convenient alternative to filling the air with savory aromas comes from the barbecue expert, Weber-Stephen Products Co., Palatine, Illinois. The Weber Genesis gas grill series offers models that feature an exclusive flavorizer system to perfectly control grilling with real cookout flavor. Unlike ordinary gas grills that collect grease in lava rocks, there are no flare-ups to worry about. Flavorizer bars laid criss-cross above the burners heat evenly, so when juices drip, they vaporize instantly, allowing the barbecue flavor to go back into the food. There are no hot or cold spots, and no charring. Both the cooking grills and the flavorizer bars are porcelain-on-steel; they are easy to clean and rust-resistant.

The Genesis collection, available in different sizes and prices, includes a Weber hallmark—a choice of direct cooking (for searing steaks, hamburgers, etc.) or indirect cooking (for roasting larger items like ham, roast, or turkey)—which is controlled by the patented ignition system that instantly lights the burners. The flame can be adjusted.

If the space is totally enclosed, gadget-conscious porch aficionados may want to have a media center innocuously designed and built into a wall area so the television, video cassette recorder, stereo, and/or disc equipment don't detract from the porchiness of the exterior room. Plan for storage space, too, with specially sized pockets and shelves built into the unit to house record albums, video and audio tapes, and compact discs.

If these sorts of playthings are too civilized for your porch presence, simply sit back and ponder the unambiguous tranquility of the great outdoors.

The High-Tech Porch

Following are some high-tech, home communications devices you may want to include on your porch:

- Selective call intercom with radio. Talk one-on-one with any station on the household system. Some models allow intercom calls while on the phone, digital display of phone numbers, cassette recorder features, and a deluxe radio. Other types have a telephone-type keypad for private, one-to-one communication—press to speak, release to listen. These have two electronic volume controls for intercom and radio.
- Built-in outdoor speakers. Weather-resistant with recess or surface mounts. Use with remote control.
- Radio intercom with built-in cassette recorder. This centralized system works as a message center, records special occasions and radio music, and plays cassettes.

Courtesy Nutone

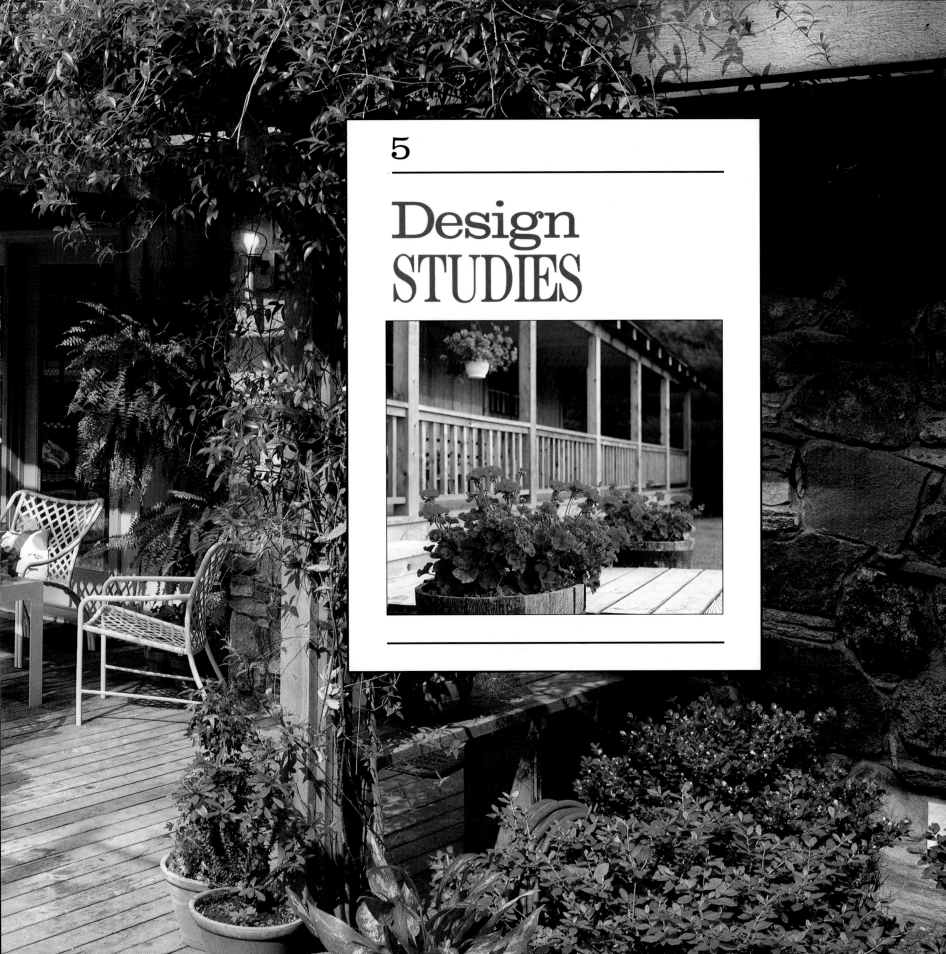

5

Design
STUDIES

© Dodo's Photos

© Dodo's Photos

THE WILKEY HOUSE
Fryeburg, Maine

When the Wilkey family moved into their two-hundred-year-old farmhouse in Fryeburg, Maine, the front facade was "screaming for a porch," said Elaine Wilkey. Although research showed the original structure had a wrap-around porch, Mrs. Wilkey had her own ideas. She felt a frontal position would better enhance the lines of the house.

Among the design ideas she assigned to a local builder was a custom-made balustrade of beveled poplar. The wooden posts were specially designed, too, and boast decorative and practical touches, such as scroll-like wind braces to help withstand blustery New England breezes. The natural-colored wooden lattice-work was purchased at the local lumber store and installed by Mr. Wilkey.

In keeping with the traditional design, Mrs. Wilkey decided on a natural, deep-grained hardwood floor that was specially treated to withstand the effects of weather.

The palette Mrs. Wilkey selected is particularly eyecatching; Cape Cod yellow for the base of the home, white trim, and burnt cranberry for the front door; the vinyl shutters painted blue are a wonderful traditional accent.

A collector of antiques, Mrs. Wilkey dresses the porch during the spring and summer with both antique and new wicker furniture and hanging pots full of blooming freesia; the wicker planter is color-coordinated with marigolds and geraniums.

While the Wilkey family enjoys using their porch for dining and just plain relaxing, neighbors seem to appreciate it too. "They stop by and tell us how much the porch has improved the home," says Mrs. Wilkey.

© Dodo's Photos

The Wilkey's farmhouse in Fryeburg, Maine reflects the homeowners design ideas and interest in antiques.

A SUMMER HOUSE

Cape Cod, Massachusetts

Spectacular views of the nearby Atlantic Ocean inspired the owners of this vacation home in Cape Cod, Massachusetts to design a second-story porch and a rooftop lookout as part of the overall house plan.

Because the porch is perched 15 feet (4.5 meters) off the ground and stands 12 feet (3.6 meters) tall with a lofty cathedral ceiling, screening it posed a challenge. The homeowners wanted to avoid normal methods that required extension ladders and scaffolding. The solution was an inexpensive, time efficient, and flexible technique that is relevant for a ground-level porch as well.

Co-owner Roy Barnhart, a magazine editor and veteran remodeler/builder, treated the open areas of the porch as if they were immense windows. He designed frames that can be installed and removed from inside the porch. Each opening is designed in such a way that every panel above and below the railing can be simply slipped into place and fastened with screw stops.

The upper screens can be put in place from the porch, and a stepladder used to secure the screens when the stops are inserted.

The key to the flexibility of this convertible porch is the removable baluster framework. Each section has a two-by-four rail screwed in place to divide the upper and lower openings. Every baluster is screwed to strips and then screw-fastened at the top and bottom.

The screen frames, installed with aluminum mesh, are constructed from one-inch (2.5-centimeters) square aluminum tubing.

The screens are in place during the summer months, when the porch functions as an exterior room for eating, sleeping, and entertaining. The spacious and stylish living-dining area opens onto the porch with a sweep of large windows and a glass door.

Designed to take advantage of the beautiful views, this home boasts a porch on the second level as well as a rooftop lookout.

THE GOODWIN HOUSE
Morristown, New Jersey

This historical home, located in Morristown, New Jersey, has been restored to maintain its Victorian character and integrates updated, weatherized materials for long-lasting wear. Designed by local architect Collins B. Weir in 1875, the house features the original enclosed front porch with adjoining gazebo.

© George Goodwin (all photos)

Homeowners Mr. and Mrs. George Goodwin enjoy the porch year-round. The original windows with movable sashes provide good light, which is especially advantageous for Goodwin, a professional photographer who often uses the room as a studio for his still-life work. In the summer the panels are easily removed and the porch converts to an open, airy room excellent for entertaining.

The Goodwins relied on the expertise of her father, John Gulick, a retired engineer, for the exterior restoration work. The major problems needing attention were the crumbling porch foundation and rotting beams. In addition, the exterior required a fresh paint job. Handyman

History and modern technology joined hands with the exterior restoration of this Morristown, New Jersey home. The original front porch is more than one hundred years old.

115

Special attention was given to the crumbling porch foundation. The original brick supports were replaced with newly doweled posts.

Gulick replaced the original brick supports with rot-resistant, pressure-treated cedar. He covered the brick foundation with a lattice-work structure purchased and modified to fit.

The Goodwins decided on a progression of earthen tints for a fresh looking exterior. The body of the house was painted light gray, the supports in a medium hue, and the windows in dark gray. The burgundy shutters are a beautiful contrast to the rest of the house; it's a visually pleasing decorating touch to bridge the interior colorations, especially the burgundy and rose shades of the rug in the foyer.

The restoration of the porch included new beams. The Goodwins enjoy their front porch and adjoining gazebo for entertaining, and occasionally use it as a photography studio.

© Robert Apte

© Robert Apte

A JAPANESE COUNTRY PORCH

Berkeley, California

The Bay Region style of this traditional Berkeley, California house is typical of many of the older homes in the area. The brown, wooden, shingled structure is situated on a hillside with beautiful vistas evoking a life-style with both casual and formal qualities.

When the homeowners turned to Ace Architects in nearby Oakland for a porch addition, the design considerations included a structure that would relate to the tradition of the Berkeley style. Also, the couple wanted a design that would reflect their interest in collecting Asian decorative arts. The unique design solution was a porch constructed in the style of a Japanese country farmhouse.

The country farmhouse approach of this porch encompasses both open and enclosed features. The rustic flavor of the pavilion serves as a bridge to the landscaped garden area.

119

The challenge of transmitting natural light into the enclosed area of the porch was accomplished with the inclusion of a tall skylight which scoops the light and bounces it into the space.

© Robert Apte

© Robert Apte

The porch addition replaced an unusable greenhouse-like exterior enclosure along the side of the house that had never been conditioned for the cold weather.

The country farmhouse approach has both open and enclosed features. The exposed rustic flavor of the pavilion area serves as a bridge to the beautifully landscaped garden area used for informal entertainment and hot tub activities. The pavilion also unites the more formal, family-oriented enclosed area with the expansion of the adjoining breakfast room.

Special details included the use of materials indigenous to the region, such as cedar for the overall construction, eucalyptus for railings and columns, and madrone, a reddish wood, for floors.

A northern exposure made a challenge of transmitting natural light into the enclosed area. This was accomplished by the installation of a tall skylight, or light scoop, which captures the light and bounces it into the space.

The West African slate lining the floor of the garden area was laid in a zig-zag fashion to heed the advice of a Japanese saying; "evil spirits travel in straight lines."

A number of other Asian influences may be seen in decorative touches such as castings for the double door hardware and door pulls from Katmandu that the couple brought back from their travels. The walls are constructed of plaster with chopped straw, which Howard says is a typical Japanese country house wall finish. To complement the design, the heated space also features unusual contemporary light fixtures made by a local Japanese artisan.

The design team that planned this porch used materials indigenous to the region; one example is the madrone (a regional wood) flooring.

SUNSPACE ADDITION

A sunspace can be an ideal addition that easily extends interior living space for year-round activities. A highly stylized enclosed porch with transparent roof and sides, the sunspace's framing is usually wood or aluminum.

There are many sunspace models and options to choose from. Width, height, slope of roof and the eave configuration—curved or angular—vary by model. There are standard size modules which can be shortened or extended to the desired dimensions.

The first preparatory step is to square and level the base of the house where the addition will be located. There are a number of important details to be handled in a precise manner, like preparing the slab for the preassembled framework.

Low-profile sizes are suitable for houses with low overhangs. The structure can be integrated into the roof line, or be attached to a corner or side of the home. When positioned in a sunny, south-facing location, it can work as a solar collector to trap the sun's heat.

The pre-engineered sunspace kits can be installed by skilled do-it-yourselfers, but experts recommend that homeowners hire a local contractor, or a manufacturer's agent experienced in such installations. Proper equipment is required to handle large lites of insulated glass and experience is invaluable in understanding the intricacies of installing foundations and other incidentals.

Pre-engineered sunspace kits should be installed by experienced professionals who have the proper equipment and know-how to handle the structure.

GREEK REVIVAL HOME
Manhasset, New York

The portico of this Greek Revival structure, located in Manhassett, New York, had a problem typical of homes built during the nineteenth century—the flooring deck was in dire need of restoration.

The restoration is especially important for this historic structure known as the Judge Horatio Gates Onderdonk House, built in 1836. The home is now the property of a local civic association, which also owns an adjoining development of 250 homes. The portico is, indeed, a formal "front door" as it welcomes association members for meetings and groups of local school children for tours of the celebrated first floor of memorabilia.

During the early phase of this porch renovation, the rotted section of the deck was cut out and replaced with pressure-treated lumber.

William Gross, a local contractor, approached the project with other exterior repairs in mind: replacement of the original tin roof and the upper ends of the columns.

During phase one, he cabled the columns together, cut out the rotted section of the decking surface, and secured the cables to the bottom of the columns on the underside of the deck. He then jacked up the whole portion of the deck. New footings were installed underneath each of the four columns along the front.

The deck's structure was then rebuilt with pressure-treated lumber, resistant to both rot and termites. The new flooring material is a tongue-and-groove fir wood.

Because the capitals had been crushed over the years, Gross replaced the four boxlike shapes and added a two-by-four component to rest between the circular ring and the base of the roof.

These photos show the replacement of the capitals, which had been crushed over the years. The outcome of this restoration is a classic, neo-Greek porch.

© William Gross (all photos)

PORCH FACELIFT
Syracuse, New York

This double porch of a Syracuse, New York home is undergoing a spring facelift.

New posts are being installed to support the roof. A major problem was that the former column bases rested directly on the porch deck, trapping moisture, which caused them to rot. The columns were replaced and a slablike

aluminum member was added at the base. It was during the preliminary inspection for repairs that the homeowners determined the roof, railings, and related woodwork had also deteriorated.

Also being replaced are newel posts for the stairs; designed in a style similar to the handrails, they will add traditional character to the older home.

A combination railing with built-in baluster in a crisscross 'X' motif provides a nice finishing touch to this repair project.

© Daniella Jo Nilva (all photos)

This porch was in desperate need of a facelift. The porch roof was sagging and the posts and stairs were rotting.

WOODEN PORCH ADDITION TO A TRADITIONAL HOME

Older homes can present a challenge when it comes to adding outdoor living spaces. There are a number of options available and you can combine and adapt several solutions to meet your needs.

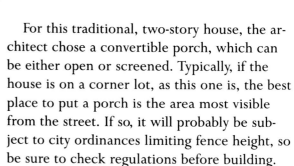

This new porch is well integrated into the design of this older home.

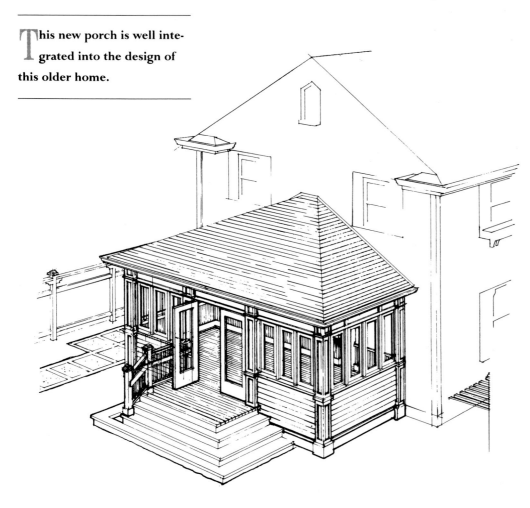

For this traditional, two-story house, the architect chose a convertible porch, which can be either open or screened. Typically, if the house is on a corner lot, as this one is, the best place to put a porch is the area most visible from the street. If so, it will probably be subject to city ordinances limiting fence height, so be sure to check regulations before building.

This porch was constructed almost entirely from wood. Its slanting roof and the stairs leading into the yard both echo the shape of the roof of the main structure, thus incorporating the new porch into the design of this older home.

A glass door leads from the porch into the house. A wooden wainscot runs the length of the interior.

If you do choose to place your porch so that it is visible from the street, you will probably want to include a fence in the design to insure some privacy. Consider a picket fence that joins with the existing shrubbery to obscure the view into the yard. If the new porch is attached to the side of the house, add thick landscape shrubbery to help provide a semi-private space. The lot's definition can be further enhanced with planters along the edge of the ground and fence boundaries. Add an arbor for additional privacy.

A LUXURIOUS PORCH ADDITION

Northwestern United States

To enjoy being outdoors, despite the frequent rains and drizzles characteristic of the North-west, the owners of this contemporary home designed an open porch with overhead protection that brilliantly blends into the landscape and garden area.

Located off the dining and kitchen areas, the outdoor room is a transitional space that's part house and part garden. The lattice and post wall structures let garden fragrances and breezes flow through, yet provide a semblance of privacy from neighboring homes.

Intending to both entertain and relax in this alfresco living space, the homeowners installed a hot tub to flank the wide open entryway. The custom-designed unit is parallel to the layout of the porch and adds a dramatic, yet functional flair to the landscape. For the garden pathway, the wooden floor planking is laid vertically and is topped with a contemporary garden bridge.

This beautiful outdoor living space is open but protected; part garden, part house.

Glossary

Here are some basic building and design terms to use as a handy reference.

BALUSTRADE. A railed structure with any number of vertical, closely spaced supports, or balusters. It usually runs along the edge of a porch and can include both a top and a bottom rail. Symmetrical baluster shapes swell toward bottom and top.

BANQUETTE. A long bench with an upholstered seat, usually along a wall.

CANTILEVER. Any rigid structural member that projects beyond its support wall or column, such as a girder, truss, or beam.

CAPITAL. The upper end of a column or pilaster, usually decorated.

CLAPBOARD. An exterior type of weatherproofed siding made of wooden boards laid horizontally for covering the outer walls of the house.

CORNICE. A prominent, continuous, projecting feature at the top of a wall; usually specially shaped.

CUPOLA. A dome shape that covers a circular or polygonal area, usually on a roof.

EASEMENT. A right held by one property owner to make use of the land of another for a limited purpose.

© Christopher Bain 1989

© Donn Young

FACADE. The front or side exterior of a building.

FANLIGHT. A window over a door or another window; usually has the form of a semicircle or half of an ellipse.

FENESTRATION. The design and disposition of windows and other exterior openings of a building.

GABLE. The portion of the front or side of a building enclosed by masking the end of a pitched roof; triangular shape that runs from the tier of the cornice to the top of the roof.

LATTICE. A structure of crossed wooden strips usually arranged to form a diagonal pattern of open spaces between the strips.

NEWEL POST. A central pillar supporting one end of a handrail at the top or bottom of a flight of stairs.

SETBACK. The distance from the front property line at which an addition can be built to a house.

VERNACULAR ARCHITECTURE. A style of building typifying the commonest techniques, decorative features, and materials of a particular historical period, region, or group of people.

WIDOW'S WALK. A platform or walk atop a roof; often used as a lookout.

Sources

ORGANIZATIONS & ASSOCIATIONS

American Institute of Architects
1735 New York Ave. NW
Washington, D.C. 20006
or contact the local AIA chapter for a
    copy of "You and Your Architect"

American Lighting Association
435 North Michigan Ave.
Chicago, IL 60611-4067
"Lighting Your Life" home lighting guide
    (Send check for $2)

Greenhouses for Living
350 Fifth Ave.
Suite 6124
New York, NY 10001

Italian Tile Center
499 Park Ave.
New York, NY 10022

National Greenhouse Manufacturers
    Association
P.O. Box 5676
Pana, IL 62557

National Pest Control Association, Inc.
8100 Oak St.
Dunn Loring, VA 22027

Remodelors Council of the National
    Association of Home Builders
15th and M Sts. NW
Washington, D.C. 20005
(Send a self-addressed, stamped envelope
    for "How to Choose a Remodeler
    Who's on the Level")

Tile Council of America
P.O. Box 326
Princeton, NJ 08542

Wall Covering Information Bureau
355 Lexington Ave.
New York, NY 10017

DESIGNERS

Referral Services

American Society of Interior Designers
Contact local chapter of ASID, or call
    ASID national headquarters at 212-
    944-9220 for information about near-
    est chapter.
("You and Your Interior Designer," a
    guide for selecting and working with
    interior designers, is available from
    ASID headquarters: 1430 Broadway,
    New York, NY 10018.)

Decorator Previews
P.O. Box 1482
Murray Hill Station
New York, NY 10156
Office locations: New York, NY; West-
    port, CT; Chicago, IL; Washington,
    D.C.; Los Angeles and San Francisco,
    CA.

Design Link
611 Broadway
Suite 623
New York, NY 10012

COLUMNS

A.F. Schwerd Manufacturing Co.
3215 McClure Ave.
Pittsburgh, PA 15212

American Wood Column Corp.
913 Grand St.
Brooklyn, NY 11211

Chadsworth, Inc.
Box 53268
Atlanta, GA 30355

Moultrie Manufacturing
Box 1179, Dept. PG17
Moultrie, GA 31776-1179

Nord Co.
Box 1187
Everett, WA 98206

RAILINGS, BALUSTERS, & SPINDLES

Gerber Industries, Inc.
P.O. Box 610
St. Peters, MO 63376

Vintage Wood Works
513 South Adams #1227
Fredericksburg, TX 78624

Weyerhaeuser Co.
3601 Minnesota Dr.
Suite 750
Bloomington, MN 55435

LATTICE

Cross Industries
3174 Marjan Dr.
Atlanta, GA 30341

Weyerhaeuser Co.
3601 Minnesota Dr. Suite 750
Bloomington, MN 55435

WINDOWS & DOORS

Andersen Corp.
Bayport, MN 55003

Atrium Door and Window Corp.
P.O. Box 226957
Dallas, TX 75222

Benchmark Doors Div.
General Products Co.
P.O. Box 7387
Fredericksburg, VA 22404

Beveled Glass Industries
6006 W. Washington Blvd.
Culver City, CA 90232

Eagle Window & Door, Inc.
375 East 9th St.
Dubuque, IA 52001

Elegant Entries
65 Water St.
Worcester, MA 01604

Fiberlux, Inc.
59 S. Terrace Ave.
Mt. Vernon, NY 10550

Hurd Millwork Co.
520 S. Whelen
Medford, WI 54451

Marvin Windows
Warroad, MN 56763

Morgan Products
P.O. Box 2446
Oshkosh, WI 54903-2446

Peachtree Windows and Doors
Box 570
Norcross, GA 30091

Pease Industries
7100 Dixie Highway
Fairfield, OH 45014

Pella/Rolscreen
100 Main St.
Pella, IA 50219

Sebastopol Window Co.
9775 Mill Station Rd.
Sebastopol, CA 95472

Silverton Victorian Millworks
P.O. Box 2987
Durango, CO 81302

Stanley Door Systems
1225 E. Maple
Tory, MI 48084

Weather Shield Manufacturing, Inc.
P.O. Box 309
Medford, WI 54451

Weathervane Window Co.
P.O. Box 2424
Kirkland, WA 98033-2424

Webb Manufacturing
1201 Maple
Conneaut, OH 44030-0707

WOOD SCREENS/ STORM DOORS & PANELS

New England Screen Door Co.
P.O. Box 128
Bristol, ME 04539

The Old Wagon Factory
P.O. Box 1427
Clarksville, VA 23927

FLOOR COVERINGS

Vinyl Tile

Allied Tile Manufacturing Corp.
2840 Atlantic Ave.
Brooklyn, NY 11207

Amtico
3131 Princeton Pike
Lawrenceville, NJ 08648

Armstrong World Industries
P.O. Box 3001
Lancaster, PA 17604

Azrock Industries, Inc.
P.O. Box 34030
San Antonio, TX 78265

GMT Floor Tile Inc.
1255 Oak Point Ave.
Bronx, NY 10474

Kentile Floors Inc.
58 Second Ave.
Brooklyn, NY 11215

NAFCO
National Floor Products Co., Inc.
P.O. Box 354
Florence, AL 35631

Tarkett, Inc.
800 Lanidex Plaza
Parsippany, NJ 07054

Sheet Vinyl

Armstrong World Industries
P.O. Box 3001
Lancaster, PA 17604

Congoleum
Ruppman Marketing Services
1909 East Cornell St.
Peoria, IL 61614

Mannington Mills Inc.
Mannington Mills Rd.
Salem, NJ 08079

Tarkett, Inc.
800 Lanidex Plaza
Parsippany, NJ 07054

Ceramic Tile

American Olean Tile Company, Inc.
1000 Cannon Ave.
Lansdale, PA 19446-0271

Atlantic Trading Co., Ltd.
P.O. Box 495
New Cumberland, PA 17070

Epro, Inc.
156 E. Broadway
Westerville, OH 43081

Glen-Gery Corp./Hanley Plant
135 Comerce Way
Summerville, PA 03801

GTE Products Corp.
Route 28
Greenland, NH 15864

Huntington Tile, Inc.
P.O. Box 1149
Corona, CA 91718

Mid-State Tile
A Mannington Co.
P.O. Box 177
Lexington, NC 27292

Quarry Tile Co.
Building 12
Spokane Industrial Park
Spokane, WA 99216

Summitville Tiles
Box 73
Summitville, OH 43962

Terra Designs
241 E. Blackwell St.
Dover, NJ 07801

Dimension Stone

Marble Institute of America
33505 State St.
Farmington, MI 48024

Hardwood/Prefinished

Bruce Hardwood Floors
16803 Dallas Parkway
Dallas, TX 75248

Hartco
Tibbals Flooring Co.
P.O. Box 1001
Oneida, TN 37841-1001

Kentucky Wood Floors
P.O. Box 33276
Louisville, KY 40232

Lindal Cedar Homes, Inc.
4300 S. 104th Pl.
Seattle, WA 98178

Mannington Wood Floors
1327-T
Lincoln Dr.
High Point, NC 27260

Robbins/Sykes, Inc.
4777 Eastern Ave.
Cincinnati, OH 45226

Wood

California Redwood Association
405 Enfrente Dr.
Suite 200
Novato, CA 94949

Southern Forest Products Association
P.O. Box 52468
New Orleans, LA 70152

Western Wood Products Association
Yeon Building
522 SW Fifth Ave.
Portland, Or 97204-2122
(Send a check for $2.00 to receive a brochure of conceptual plans called "Outdoor Space: Western Lumber Projects That Make it Work")

Outdoor Carpet

General Felt Industries
Park 80 Plaza
West-1
Saddlebrook, NJ 07662

Sheridan Carpet Mills
P.O. Box 1627
Dalton, GA 30722

Sisal & Coir Matting

Phoenix Carpet
979 Third Ave.
New York, NY 10022

Rosecore Carpet Co.
979 Third Ave.
New York, NY 10022

Alison T. Seymour, Inc.
5423 W. Marginal Way S.W.
Seattle, WA 98106

WOOD STOVES

Ceramic Radiant Heat
Pleasant Dr.
Lochmere, NH 03252

Hearthstone Corp., Inc.
Hearthstone Way
Morrisville, VT 05661

Martin Industries
P.O. Box 128
Florence, AL 35631

Vermont Castings, Inc.
Prince St.
Randolph, VT 05060

PELLET STOVES

Martin Industries
P.O. Box 128
Florence, AL 35631

Pyro Industries
11625 Airport Rd.
Everett, WA 98204

Thermic, Inc.
P.O. Box 11986
Spokane, WA 99211

CEILING FANS

Emerson Builder Products
Division of Emerson Electric Co.
8400 Pershall Rd.
Hazelwood, MO 63042

Homestead Products
114 14th St.
P.O. Box 9000
Ramona, CA 92065

Hunter Fan Co.
2500 Frisco Ave.
Memphis, TN 38114

NuTone
Madison and Red Banks Rds.
Cincinnati, OH 45201

EXTERIOR LIGHTING FIXTURES & BULBS

Arroyo Craftsman
2080 Central Ave.
Building B
Duarte, CA 91010

Bega
1005 Mark Ave.
Carinteria, CA 93013

General Electric
Nela Park
Cleveland, OH 44102

Georgian Art Lighting Designs
P.O. Box 325
Lawrenceville, GA 30246

GTE Products Corp.
Sylvania Lighting Center
900 Endicott St.
Danvers, MA 01923

Hadco
Craftlite, Inc.
P.O. Box 128
100 Craftway
Littlestown, PA 17340

Kim Lighting (landscape)
16555 East Gale Ave.
City of Industry, CA 91745

North American Philips Corp.
P.O. Box 6800
Somerset, NJ 00875

Osram Corp.
110 Bracken Rd.
Montgomery, NY 12549

Poulsen Lighting Inc.
5407 N.W. 163rd St.
Miami, FL 33014

Technolite (custom)
1802 First St.
San Fernando, CA 91340

OUTDOOR/CASUAL FURNITURE & ACCESSORIES

Synthetic Resins

Allibert, Inc.
1200 Highway 27 S.
Stanley, NC 28164

Grosfillex
USA:
   Eastern Division Office
   Muhlenberg Industrial Mall
   4201 Pottsville Pike
   Reading, PA 19605

   Western Division Office
   319 Lambert St.
   Oxnard, CA 93030

CANADA:
   465 Milner Ave.
   Unit 1
   Scarborough-Ontario M1B 2K4

Triconfort
1512 Crossbeam Dr.
Suite 1000
Charlotte, NC 28217

Aluminum/Tubular & Extrusion

Brown Jordan Co.
9860 Gidley St.
P.O. Box 5688
El Monte, CA 91734

Homecrest Industries, Inc.
Box 350
Wadena, MN 56482

Meadowcraft Casual Furniture
P.O. Box 1357
Birmingham, AL 35201

Samsonite Furniture Co.
Samsonite Blvd.
Murfreesboro, TN 37133-0189

Telescope Casual Furniture, Inc.
Church St.
Granville, NY 12832

Tropitone Furniture Co.
P.O. Box 3197
Sarasota, FL 34230

Winston Furniture Co.
P.O. Box 868
Haleyville, AL 35565

Cast Aluminum

Brown Jordan
9860 Gidley St.
P.O. Box 5688
El Monte, CA 91734

Moultrie Manufacturing Co.
Moultrie, GA 31776-1179

Veneman
A Tropitone Company
P.O. Box 3197
Sarasota, FL 34230

Wrought-Iron

Lyon-Shaw
Division of Winston Furniture Company
P.O. Box 2069
Salisbury, NC 28145

Maitland-Smith
651 Ward Ave.
High Point, NC 27260

Meadowcraft Casual Furniture
P.O. Box 1357
Birmingham, AL 35201

Wicker & Rattan

Bielecky Brothers, Inc.
306 East 61st St.
New York, NY 10021

Brown Jordan
9860 Gidley St.
P.O. Box 5688
El Monte, CA 91734

Ficks Reed Co.
4900 Charlemar Dr.
Cincinnati, OH 45227

The Lane Co., Inc.
Venture Division
Altavista, VA 24517-0151

Lloyd/Flanders
3010 Tenth St.
Menominee, MI 49858-0500

Maitland-Smith
651 Ward Ave.
High Point, NC 27260

O'Asian Designs
1100 W. Walnut
Compton, CA 90020

Palecek
P.O. Box 225
Station A
Richmond, CA 94808

Pier 1 Imports
301 Commerce St.
Suite 600
Fort Worth, TX 76102

The Trading Co.
P.O. Box 6191
Vero Beach, FL

Un Jardin En Plus
425 Fairfield Ave.
Stamford, CT 06942

Molded PVC

Florida Pipe Furniture
826 Haddonfield Rd.
Cherry Hill, NJ 08002

Steel

Homecrest Industries, Inc.
Box 350
Wadena, MN 56482

Winterthur Museum and Gardens
(Gift and Garden Sampler Catalog)
Winterthur, DE 19735

Wood

Barlow Tyrie, Inc.
Subsidiary of Barlow Tyrie Ltd., Braintree,
    England
65 Great Valley Parkway
Malvern, PA 19355

Bilhuber Inc. (custom)
19 East 65th St.
New York, NY 10021

Copeland & Sons
Pierson Industrial Park
Bradford, VT 05033

Mary K. Darrah Antiques
33 Ferry St.
New Hope, PA 18938

Lister (teak)
British-American Marketing Services Ltd.
251 Welsh Pool Rd.
Lyonville, PA 19353

Masterworks (bent willow)
P.O. Box M
Marietta, GA 30061

Weatherend Estate Furniture
Imagineering, Inc.
P.O. Box 648
374 Main St.
Rockland, ME 04841

PAINTS, FINISHES, & STAINS

Benjamin Moore
51 Chestnut Ridge Rd.
Montvale, NJ 07645
(Call local dealer)

Flood Company
P.O. Box 399
Hudson, OH 44236-0399

Fuller O'Brien Paints
450 East Grand Ave.
South San Francisco, CA 94080

Glidden Co.
925 Euclid Ave.
Cleveland, OH 44115

Imperial Paint Co.
2526 N.W. Yeon
Portland, OR 97210

Olympic Stain
2233 112 Ave., N.E.
Bellevue, WA 95066

Pittsburgh Paint
PPG Industries
1 PPG Plaza
Pittsburgh, PA 15272

Pratt & Lambert Inc.
P.O. Box 22
Buffalo, NY 14240

Sherwin-Williams Company
101 Prospect Ave., N.W.
Cleveland, OH 44115

HEATING/VENTILATION

Infloor Heating Systems
920 Hamel Rd.
Hamel, MN 55340

Kool-O-Matic Corporation
1831 Terminal Rd.
Niles, MI 49120

SECURITY SYSTEMS & INTERCOMS

NuTone
Madison and Red Banks Rds.
P.O. Box 1580
Cincinnati, OH 45201

FABRICS

Brunschwig & Fils
75 Virginia Rd.
P.O. Box 905
North White Plains, NY 10603

Cohama
1407 Broadway
New York, NY 10018

Collins & Aikman
Chase Hill Rd.
Ashway, RI 02891

Covington Fabrics
267 Fifth Ave.
New York, NY 10016

Cowtan & Trout, Inc.
979 Third Ave.
New York, NY 10022

Greef Fabrics, Inc.
150 Midland Ave.
Port Chester, NY 10572

Laura Ashley
1300 MacArthur Blvd.
Mahwah, NJ 07430

Lee Jofa, Inc.
800 Central Ave.
Carlstadt, NJ 07072

Rose Cumming Chintzes Ltd.
232 East 59th St.
New York, NY 10022

Rosecore
979 Third Ave.
New York, NY 10022

F. Schumacher & Co.
79 Madison Ave.
New York, NY 10016

Stroheim & Romann
155 East 56th St.
New York, NY 10022

Waverly
79 Madison Ave.
New York, NY 10016

WINDOW TREATMENTS

HunterDouglas
2 Park Way & Route 17 South
Upper Saddle River, NJ 07458

Kirsch Division
Cooper Industries Inc.
309 N. Prospect St.
Sturgis, MI 49091

Levolor Lorentzen, Inc.
150 Lackawanna Ave.
Parsippany, NJ 07054

LouverDrape
1100 Colorado Ave.
Santa Monica, CA 90401

Awnings

Annual Awning Buyers Guide available
    from:
Awning Division
Industrial Fabrics Association
    International
345 Cedar St.
Suite 450
St. Paul, MN 55101

WALL COVERINGS

Columbus Wall Covering
117 North Long Beach Rd.
Rockville Center, NY 11570

Funwall of America
3044 Northwoods Circle
Norcross, GA 30071

General Wall Covering
10 Bloomfield Ave.
Pinebrook, NJ 07058

I. Lappin Wall Covering Co., Inc.
12 Channel St.
Boston, MA 02210

Imperial Wall Coverings
23645 Mercantile Rd.
Cleveland, OH 44122

J. Josephson, Inc.
20 Horizon Blvd.
South Hackensack, NJ 07606

Schumacher
F. Schumacher & Co.
79 Madison Ave.
New York, NY 10016

Stroheim & Romann
155 East 56th St.
New York, NY 10022

Waverly
79 Madison Ave.
New York, NY 10016

Paneling

Georgia-Pacific
133 Peachtree St. N.E.
Atlanta, GA 30303

Pacific Lumber Co.
100 Shoreline Highway
Suite 125
Mill Valley, CA 94941

BARBECUES

Weber-Stephen Products Co.
200 East Daniels Rd.
Palatine, IL 60067

PLANTERS

The Alsto Company
P.O. Box 1267
Galesburg, IL 61401

Gardener's Eden
Williams-Sonoma
P.O. Box 7307
San Francisco, CA 94120-7307

Ringer
9959 Valley View Rd.
Eden Prairie, MN 55344-3585

Smith & Hawken
25 Corte Madera
Mill Valley, CA 94941

Index

Additional Photo Credits